'*We the Parasites* is my new favourite bc
of the erotics of criticism, riven with k..
sensibility. A.V. Marraccini stops you in your tracks, urges you to think
with her a while about the delicious joy of art, how we grow huge and
terrifying on it, and how this thievery, this parasitism is necessary both
for its continuance and for our own.'

— Lauren Elkin, author of *Flâneuse: Women Walk The City*

'In 1964, Sontag wrote: 'In place of a hermeneutics we need an erotics
of art.' Since then, many works of criticism have paid lip service to this
desideratum, but few have managed to achieve it. [...] In *We the Parasites*,
encountering a work of art is not fixed as a safe looking at, but rather
as an eating, a kissing, a being-seduced-by, a being-contaminated by,
a being-infected-by that restores art and criticism to the dangerous
adventure that it is.'

— Ryan Ruby

We The Parasites

Beyond Criticism Editions explores the new paths that criticism might take in the 21st century.

We encourage any kind of formal adventure: analytical, aphoristic, archival, autobiographical, citational, confessional, descriptive, dialogical, dramatic, fantastical, fictive, graphic, historical, imaginative, ironical, metaphysical, miscellaneous, mythical, palimpsestic, parasitical, philosophical, poetical, polemical, political, probational, riddling, theological, theoretical, ventriloquial.

Our only criterion is that it *discovers*.

The series is curated by Katharine Craik (Oxford Brookes University) and Simon Palfrey (Oxford University)

We The Parasites

by A. V. Marraccini

BOILER HOUSE PRESS

Beyond Criticism Editions

Contents

PART 1

1.

Here's a weird thing about some kinds of figs: there are male and female figs. The fig is an inverted flower, which needs to be pollinated to make the fig fruit that we eat. There are male and female fig wasps. The female fig wasp burrows into the male fig, called the caprifig, and the process, in turn, is called caprification, when she lays eggs and those eggs hatch. The hatchlings are blind, flightless males and young females. They have incestuous sex. The now pregnant female wasps, the ones Aristotle and Theophrastus call *psenes*, burst out of the skin of the caprifig and go off to burrow anew into other figs. Both erroneously thought this was a kind of spontaneous wasp generation, but to be fair the actual mechanism is hard to discern such that the biology of it is still a topic now.

The female fig needs to be pollinated to fruit. Bees can't do this, nor wind, because the inverted flower is sealed up inside itself. So sometimes a female wasp doesn't crawl into a male fig, where she can lay eggs. Sometimes she crawls into a female fig, where she starves and dies, but in the process pollinates the inverted flower, which can then fruit. The body of the wasp is absorbed by the growing flesh of the fig. You do eat it, in a sense, but you wouldn't know if I hadn't told you.

This is called *commensalism*, a form of parasitism in which the parasite doesn't actively harm the host. More properly, it's even a *mutualism*, dead wasps and male fig husks aside, because the fig and the wasp need each other to reproduce.

2.

I am somehow reading Updike's *The Centaur*, which makes me think this is what it must be like to be the caprifig, the male fig the female wasp lays eggs in:

"The pain extended a feeler into his head and unfolded its wet wings along the walls of his thorax, so he felt, in his sudden scarlet blindness, to be himself a large bird waking from sleep... The pain seemed to be displacing with its own hairy segments his heart and lungs..."

3.

But I'm not the fig, I'm the wasp. I burrow into sweet, dark places of fecundity, into novels and paintings and poems and architectures, and I make them my own. I write criticism, I lay it in little translucent eggs. ερινασμός. Caprification. Criticism is a mutualism as parasites like me go, or at least a commensalism, pollinating novels to make more novels; Winckelmann's halls of beautiful young men in Greek sculpture making the hot breath of living beautiful young men into *bildungsroman*, which in turn end up in marble of their own. The critical gaze is tearing apart, clawing into the soft central flesh of the tree bud.

The critical gaze is also erotic; we want things, we are by a degree of separation pollinating figs with other figs by means of our wasp bodies, rubbing two novels together like children who make two dolls "have sex", except we'll die inside the fruit and someone else will read it and eat it, rich with all the juices of my corpse. This is an odd but sensuous thing to want. And though the male-female figs exist, and the male-female wasps, the whole process, the generative third body in the dark recesses of the inverted flower, is somehow queer. Criticism, too, is queer in this way, generative outside the two-gendered model, outside the matrimonial light of day way of reproducing people, wasps, figs, or knowledge.

4.

I lied when I said I was "somehow" reading *The Centaur*. I'm reading it because one of the people who taught me, who formed me into a wasp instead of a bee or a wind, had just read it. He says it is about fathers and sons, about being both. I will never be either. I think about Chiron and Achilles, rather than Prometheus, to whom the novel refers.

Chiron, the centaur, was responsible for the education of Achilles. Patroclus, too, though he seems to have more or less tagged along for the ride. Anyhow, Achilles thinks of Chiron as a sort of father, at least in Statius, where Achilles sleeps entwined around Chiron's shoulders. There are numerous paintings of this, the education out in the rocky woods. It is no surprise they are often homoerotic— the beautiful young man, still soft before the great war at Troy, made keen-edged by the older, fiercer, inhuman centaur. The frisson as Chiron leans over Achilles, bowstring taut with an arrow about to loose!

You don't become a fig wasp on the flanks of the neo-classical tradition without having inhabited it, parasitized it yourself first as practice. This is an education. You tell yourself you are Achilles (or sometimes, Patroclus), you rationalize your world with these models, themselves parasitic on a tradition that you did not yourself make. You learn to be by being them, by pushing into them and unfolding your wet wings.

This displacement makes me shiver, a kind of longing by proxy. You learn to be an aesthete by honing everything out in some wilderness, where no one sees your missteps, your clumsy formation. I will never be a father or a son. I am not yet Chiron, but I have been Achilles. An education in this way is good practice for being a critic, for inhabiting and bursting out of galls and personae like the *psenes*.

The critical education, the mapping and re-mapping of the self onto the others of art or canonical literature, onto the Achilleses hanging ripe and easy on the trees, this, too, is an erotics. For everyone you could possibly be, for knowing how to be, for being taught how to know in this way that feels forbidden, queer, like an ekphrasis of somebody else's kiss on somebody else's vase, for the remove makes it only sweeter. You need a centaur to teach you how to both inhabit and step outside your own human-ness, to make it that contrafactual, malleable stone, and quick as a horse's rear legs jutting out of the marble of a metope.

Hence, Chiron. Hence, Achilles. Hence, myself on a cold November afternoon, looking for something in Updike by sheer force of will, of wanting to be the sort of person who can find it, those crystalline-soft particles of pollen. Learning to be a parasite is the crucible of unmet longing for that something-else that can complete you, enfolded somewhere, still perhaps hidden.

5.

My first kiss was the Nike of Samothrace.

I had self-enchanted, or rather lured a flock of wasps to my fresh, young marrow, just beginning to grow into the pulp of things. I did what anyone does when they are discovering anything about themselves of a monumentality that requires consultation; I read all the books I could get my hands on. I didn't, then, know any centaurs.

Anyway, on a day walking, just like this, across a field of high-bladed grass in the rain, a day on which I noticed the absence of oak trees, because of course, Troy, the oak in the field of battle. Because all the eggs injected into me had burst open into a thousand tiny worms and they formed the river of the Scamander mid-Oregon, because it was the first bloom of having been parasitized, the way they map and feed each onto the other. Reading does that to you; Simone Weil made me want to be anorexic. M. F. K. Fisher made me want to eat. They are parasites, too, the dead-sweet voices, the whole succulent kingdom of the shades. When I saw people do lines of cocaine off a mirror for the first time, an oddly encumbered and large wall contrivance with a protruding frame, there I was, Lucy Honeychurch without a (of course) Baedeker. If it was beautiful, being turned into one of those ants in which a fungus grows, until it runs the brain of the ant, like a zombie machine, it was also a bit obvious and teenaged, which I was, fungal-ant-stuttering-walking across the plain.

When we got there she had taken so many Vicodin, enough that she couldn't quite feel the surface of her skin, where the nerves ended. There was a black light, and she had a white wrap dress, with pleats around the chest in perpendicular folded lines. She was dancing right under the bulb when I saw the man first touch her skin. I tried to warn her, but she was somewhere else. Hands grabbing.

The white dress in the light, moving as wind blew it back. Even as I saw it I knew: the statue with the arms thrown asunder, headless, acephale, ecstatic but also broken and therefore unmade. Later, too, I would see this in the white of a Twombly triptych in Berlin, Thrysis of Etna (born with a tuneful voice!). Just then, though, Twombly hadn't hatched yet. But the Greeks had, and Forster's Greeks too, the ones who realize things, boys with their hands in the smalls of each other's backs.

I turned and ran back across the grass in the rain. I lay down in one of her bunk beds and pretended to sleep. She came in hours later, and by way of apology, crawled into bed with me, shifted the strands of my damp hair, and kissed me, just the once, for long so desired, and yet, I kept silent, trembling, and lay with my eyes still closed, my breath dactylic, long short short fast. On the airplane back I told myself to *Lay your sleeping head my love / Human on my faithless* arm for her, for me, as if by saying it Auden was me and was speaking for her, for me, doing what hadn't been done. The *psenes* burst out of me as ventriloquisms, juvenilia, poetry. Then they disappeared, dissipated into the air. For now, for then.

Every queer person I know has this story, their First, but mine was more a mythos, a more story-like story than anyone else's I had ever heard. This is what happens when you get too close to art, undiluted, when criticism isn't there. It lays its eggs in you. It breeds. It becomes your first kiss, your first lover, your first experience of everything before you even open your eyes. It is there, coursing along in your blood like a pleasing contaminate you can't ever filter out. Of course you are Achilles, of course the thorax of your pain is creeping and deathly, of course you have been reified by already existing in the world. You yourself are only made real by the precondition of the story of you, inscribed, parasitically, permanently, deathless god with eyes blank like butter. You contemplate, at some point, if you are merely somebody else's, a dead author's perhaps, a *psen*, laid in the fig of a book.

Criticism usurps the kiss of the reader's mouth to the novel, the viewer's to the painted panel. We snatch kisses up in between and filter them, making our own weird honey. Now that I'm a critic, it's safe. I don't look to Homer directly, to weep and burn my own hair. I look askance. I don't want to be a marionette on his strings again, to be animated by my too-close parasites, my chosen ones, my comforters and bedfellows. I need to be buffered.

But still; the feeling of being buffeted directly is sharp, human, pleasing. A kiss on the lips. A bite, even. And she is still for me, there, my Nike of Samothrace. An education makes me say it wryly, but tonight in the rain, there is no more wryness there; I am unprotected by the mechanisms of my critical-academical position. I wait to feel the wound, the one the mosquito numbs when it sucks at you. I want it.

6.

I don't like mosquitos very much in reality, but what I dislike more are ticks. I loathe them, in fact. Though in the same childhood summer I got stung on a sandaled foot by six hornets, what I came to fear more, in the long span of things, were ticks.

Ticks have a mechanism for when they get full. They eventually stop feeding and sit there menacingly, white globuled kernels like the rows on uncooked corn. Just shells of bodies, ballooned up with blood.

I don't think I have that mechanism, for books or for art. Someday I will be feeding away, mouth to flank, hand to page, or sitting in the upper balcony of the ballet, and I'll explode and the thin walls of my body will seep out faintly remembered, slightly digested prose. Everyone will look away politely, and disinfect with their portable hand sanitizer.

To get ticks off a dog, I once saw a counselor at summer camp put a cigarette lighter to the ends of them. This cannot be the best way to do it, but perhaps the tick, on threat of death, will abandon its parasitic, stable host and unclamp.

What is the cigarette lighter for criticism?

7.

The opposite of a centaur who is not Chiron is a Lapith. Centaurs, you see, are normally not like Chiron, they are like me, like the ticks, a bit feral. They can't control their impulses like the Lapiths, the humans who invited them to a wedding. The resulting battle, called the Centauromachy, is fundamentally this: the humans vs. the impulses which we choose to characterize as non-human, desirous, dangerous.

Of course, when we fight our own unbridled desire is it not also implicitly erotic? Deadly wrestling, blood, spit, tears, bodies manneristically in exaggerated curvature displayed. My favorite of the Lapith and Centaur metopes at the British Museum has no head on either figure, it's all grist and muscle and bone, pulling in chiasmatic bursts across drapery and hooved legs. This gallery is where Alec and Maurice meet, I think, in Forster's novel by the same name, where Alec is going to supposedly blackmail him for being gay. They end up fucking in a hotel room instead. In the Merchant Ivory film the background is the Assyrian and Babylonian reliefs, which works less well.

Achilles learns not to be like the metope centaurs, paradoxically, from a centaur, from Chiron, who is a barbarian more civilized than the civil. He outdoes the Lapiths, and Lord Elgin, and me, *bar bar*, because I actually think it would have been more interesting if the centaurs had won, and it wasn't all some big propagandistic allegory for 5th century Athens, the proto-Cold War, empire, and a movie about getting with your friend's gardener. I claim this but I love those metopes, I sit on them getting fat with marmoreal blood. A better critic would remind you how small they actually are, how fractured, the complicated intertwinings of their specious purchase from the Turks, the validity of the claims of the current Greeks.

I just sit there being sort of jealous, actually, at my own remove, my own incapacity for an ecstatic godly possession, like in the *Ion*, Plato's *Ion*, when poetry just flows out of you like a chain of magnets from the gods. I'm too boring for an *ecstasos*. I just watch other people's, other centaurs' and write about it, the dissolved chitin of the wasp you can't taste, really, inside the fig. The best and most skilled of parasites live, reproduce, and die, without their hosts every really knowing, or at least being able to do anything about it. I'm not even a good parasite because painters or novelists can see me seeing them, drawing off their vital fluid, forming new and odd things in my dark-lobed ovarians, and then shoving them out, hastily and fitfully, into the world of papers and reviews.

Well, whoever carved this metope is dead. He can't see me, sitting here, eating his shade; an ekphrasis, engorgement. Little wet-winged wasplings— we don't need to cross the three rivers to the kingdom of the dead, we don't need any golden laurel branches, we don't even save coins under our tongues for the ferryman. The advantage of being a buzzing *psen* is that you can flit between dead artists and live ones, long-dissipated slime molded corpses of poets and the guy you just heard read over cocktails, without anybody noticing. How uncivilized. The dead all love me. Now for the living.

8.

H. D., in her poem "Cities", writes about bees, not wasps, but I think she knows me and my dead lovers, my lovely prey, the imaginaries we make as intimate little gifts in the dark to ourselves, between ourselves and art:

> Though they sleep or wake to torment
> and wish to displace our old cells— thin r
> are gold—
> that their larvae grow fat—
> is our task the less sweet? Though we wander about,
> find no honey of flowers in this waste, is
> our task the less sweet—
> who recall the old splendour,
> await the new beauty of cities?

The city is peopled
with spirits, not ghosts, O my love:

Though they crowded between and usurped the kiss of my mouth
their breath was your gift,
their beauty, your life.

9.

When I saw the white of Twombly's panels in her dress, I was not the only one. Consider this excerpt from Twombly's Wikipedia page:

Phaedrus incident

In 2007, an exhibition of Twombly's paintings, Blooming, a Scattering of Blossoms and Other Things, and other works on paper from gallerist Yvon Lambert's collection, was displayed from June to September at the Museum of Contemporary Art in Avignon . On July 19, 2007, police arrested Cambodian-French artist Rindy Sam after she kissed one panel of Twombly's triptych Phaedrus. The panel, an all-white canvas, was smudged by Sam's red lipstick and she was tried in a court in Avignon for "voluntary degradation of a work of art".

Sam defended her gesture to the court: "J'ai fait juste un bisou. C'est un geste d'amour, quand je l'ai embrassé, je n'ai pas réfléchi, je pensais que l'artiste, il aurait compris... Ce geste était un acte artistique provoqué par le pouvoir de l'art" ("It was just a kiss, a loving gesture. I kissed it without thinking; I thought the artist would understand...

It was an artistic act provoked by the power of art").

The prosecution described the act as a "sort of cannibalism, or parasitism", but admitted that Sam was "visibly not conscious of what she has done", asking that she be fined €4,500 and compelled to attend a citizenship class. The art work was worth an estimated $2 million. In November 2007, Sam was convicted and ordered to pay €1,000 to the painting's owner, €500 to the Avignon gallery where it was exhibited, and €1 to the painter.

"J'ai fait juste un bisou" !!!

The white on Twombly's three panels in Berlin, about Thyrsis of Etna, was the white I saw first in his work that moved me. The work itself is a sort of cannibalism or parasitism on Theocritus, the song of one shepherd mourning the death of another, part of which Twombly scrawls in his thin, uneven hand. Most of the panel is this white, the absence of the dead beloved that is the mourning.

To be a critic and to be queer both are exercises in denial, in misplaced longing, in usurpation of kisses of the mouth. H. D. knew, hanging off the fat shaggy thighs of a Homeric ram, lapping around its head severed at the altar, a hecatomb of rams, of bulls. Twombly, too, differently, exists in the space where the head used to be, and the kind of gods who like heads and arterial red, but can be so unkind to both commentary and, because it is in a sense the ultimate comment, wanting. I live, temporarily, in a state of Twombly white, when I am a wasp without a fig.

"C'est un geste d'amour"

Find no honey or flowers in this waste.

10.

Tonight, at a party, the Centauromachy surrounded me. I was in a Gentlemen's Club in Pall Mall, an old classic, the Traveller's Club, which admits women only for parties. I *know* I *know*, but listen, there was this frieze I wanted to see, from plaster casts of the Temple of Apollo at Bassae. There I was jostling between men in variations on Eton ties, spilling white wine on my knuckles, my one band-aided middle finger, staring up like I didn't know the ending, that the Lapiths win, that they drive the last of the centaurs up into caves in mountain redoubts where they still live.

It was like a giant Jasperware plate, these blue Wedgewood things you see in antique stores, with white classical figures on them, an imitation of the Portland Vase, I think, and popular in the 19th century. I bought an ashtray of one from a place called Antiques Mall Y'All near US 1, the big highway, just south of Miami, Florida, with my parents, when I was still in school. I didn't smoke, I just liked to stroke the figures and pretend at *Brideshead Revisited*.

That ashtray is still in my childhood bedroom somewhere. I will probably see it for the holidays. I think it was in the implausible shape of a heart. As for the frieze, people were saying it was from the Parthenon, but that's a lot bigger, actually, and the Lapith-Centaur part is the *metope*, a different part of the building— and oh it doesn't matter how I know these things. It's that they come out of me as if you hired a monkey for a party, a showpiece on a chain, and it suddenly started to talk, that's how these kinds of people look at me when I tell them about the Centauromachy, or the frieze, which is a metope, or a different frieze entirely.

One of the older men, not unkindly, asks me what the young people these days are reading, what the last poetry I read was that moved me.

"Theocritus, last night, but I mean that hardly co —"

"Oh. *Really*. Oh my then, well Theocritus! Yes."

It's like you've hit them with some sort of bomb, the bomb of you, this little American girl with a high voice on about Theocritus. It's like you shouldn't exist really, the talking monkey. Or maybe you've just been educated by centaurs and that makes you extra-human somehow, scary. I'm frightening or bewitching to them, these men, and they either are shaken somehow and move away, or inexplicably take a deep interest in asking me, for the next thirty minutes or so, how I came to be.

What I want to say is this: my mother she slept with a god, you know, or my father. I'm a bit strange 'round the edges. I used to be a sheep. Or a tree. How pastoral. The Theocritus I was reading was for Twombly, for Thyrsis of Etna, but that's the one in Berlin I think of, about death, with the black rent in the middle, the faintest hints of blue and red, and the line in Twombly's scrabbled-scratch hand, *born with a tuneful voice*.

Afterward, though, something changed, and this man, this very old man, who I thought had been introduced as simply "Gary"— an odd thing at such a party but who was I to know?— recited some poems from memory. There was Larkin, and Frost, and then Graves, this Robert Graves, something about the cruelties of November, the muse ungirded in her robes shivering for winter. He means himself, too, the November of his life. He says he may have one more book in him, but his legs have failed him, well only the left. He sits in a chair, fragile.

Then, as if very tired, he takes two walking sticks around his wrists, clinical ones that end in hooves, and leaves. He is a wounded centaur now, and he leaves the battle for his cave high in a glade somewhere.

And then I'm on the Tube home really, and have only my own silence, the way Updike saw a dull girl in George Caldwell's class in *The Centaur*.

Dumb. Dumb as pure white lead.

Twombly white, lead white, the kind of dumb that speaks volumes really, that gathers in the throat and the unplayed syrinx. Updike's George was a centaur too, they exist in quietly suffering high school teachers who love their aesthete sons. They exist now, centaurs. We transplant them, like pollen on the legs of fig wasps. The neo-neo-neo-classical, we need it to be there, like a distancing frame, so we don't all go lead-dumb at the thing.

The man, it seems after hearing the name more clearly, was not Gary, but Lord Gowrie, who since receiving a heart transplant, has more than once been close to dead. He knew Robert Lowell, once. The real frieze of the Temple of Apollo at Bassae is now in the British Museum. Lord Cockrell took it in 1815, and that is how his casts of it are at his club.

Again, Updike's voice now, my inescapable Americanisms, assume (naif! idiot naif!) the man was named Gary, because somehow a random man named Gary made more sense than a hereditary seat, because Gary was someone's dad's name, a regionally successful trial lawyer or a guy who owned car dealerships, Hondas and Buicks. A guy from Alton, maybe, or like *The Centaur*'s George, from Passaic, New Jersey.

"You don't like women," she said. It seemed to be a discovery that did not excite her... The goddess became pensive. "Your trust in us is touching. What have we done to deserve our worshippers?"

"It is not what the gods do that makes us adore them," he recited. "It is that they are."

But are they? In the first of Theocritus' *Idylls*, Thyrsis

is being asked by some other shepherds to sing about the death of his friend, Daphnis. If he sings he will be given goats and a bowl, a two-handled bowl called a *kissubion*, the decoration of which the poem then goes on to describe in detail. It's ekphrastic. A step removed. The plaster casts on the wall, still another. The frieze itself, in a still small room off the Elgin marbles, are the gods there?

They've had to be. I've made them out in Jasperware.

Updike again, intruding:

... In the beginning," the centaur said, "black winged Night was courted by the wind, and laid a silver egg in the womb of

Darkness. From this egg hatched Eros, which means—?

Which means love but also lust, desire, need, want. A silver egg, which the Night, unfurling her wings lay in the dark pit of the fig, in the enfolded flowers. Night needs the Wind to make the egg. We need our re-worked gods, our ashtray divinities, a glimpse at a frieze, a pile of unread books, a large black mark in the center panel and three to the right in the Twombly gallery in the Hamburger-Banhof Museum.

11.

There was recently a theft at a museum in Dresden. The heist took place in the Grünes Gewölbe, the Green Vault, which sounds like a stand of trees curving into a nave in the forest near Bassae, but is really a state museum with the treasures of the electors of Saxony, amongst other things. The thieves cut the power and the backup alarms, hoisted themselves through a tiny window, and are seen on camera in the vault, standing in front of the faintly gilded rocaille cases in the dark. The black and white marble floors shine in the scant light of their torches and they begin to pry at the glass meant to hold them back from the diamonds.

Heists like this aren't usually for moving objects on the black market, since the jewel encrusted sword and the like are too singular to fence. They were grabbed for someone who wanted them, a Russian oligarch perhaps, who would secret them away in his basement den forever, perhaps for certain confidants and guests to see in an act of profligacy as much as intimidation.

The floors, those black and white floors, and the reflection off the glass, make the security footage look unreal, like the film *Last Year At Marienbad*. I tell myself what an awful thing this is, how this is not the desire that I have for art, the desire to secret it away in some orifice-lair like a great wyrm. Like *Marienbad* though, things are uncertain, time bulges and dilutes, and I can never be sure what is lying. This is eros, too, the hit of each sharp-tongued instrument until the pane pulls away like a net.

Updike, the failings of my body in the sharp light of his misogyny, and needing Updike anyway, is like robbing jewels. I take them as an act of eros, of profligacy, those paragraphs from *The Centaur*, secret them away in a locked room. Consider how Updike's Venus describes the gods, cruel and imperfect:

... Cheeks brow and throat flushed, she shouted toward Heaven, "Yes, Brother: blasphemy! Your gods, listen to them—a prating bluestocking, a filthy crone smelling of corn, a thieving tramp, a drunken queer, a despicable, sad, grimy, grizzled, crippled, cuckolded tinker—"

Consider the parasites that eat off the tongues of fishes, *Cymothoa exigua*, known sometimes as fish-louses. They swim into the gills, and then sever the major blood vessels at the root of the tongue, gnawing away at the flesh until they are the tongue to the fish. They live this way until the fish dies, eating scraps, being tongues. I latch onto the tongue of Theocritus sometimes. I've stolen Homer and Herodotus, too. I'm a bluestocking and broken and sometimes drunken and, yes, queer. I can hear Updike now, the words he saves for sagging female flesh, I say them to myself in the mirror. It's no good though, I've already bitten off his tongue at the root and started to speak with it, stolen it like it was already mine, shadows playing on the empty vault of the mouth, the soft palate and jawing bone. I've stolen him and his words and I've grown my flesh to them in a graft I can't undo for love or money either.

I'm a thief; a thousand hundred generations of starving Sicilian farmers indenturing their backs to some steep, rocky crag, a thousand hundred shtetl girls married off young. I'm from a flat hot suburb of a third-rate city near a swamp and the sea, I'm nothing from nowhere to you. I've seen the asphalt burble in the heat before a thunderstorm in the summer. Do you think that there are barbarians? That I am one? Well, *barbar* then. Nothing can scare me. I lived in the mouths of fishes. I lived between teeth. I ring my neck with them like the lost diamonds of Saxony as I eye Updike's patrician nose in a photograph.

Updike's homophobia was horrible, too, when he wrote of Alan Hollinghurst in 1999 in the *New Yorker* that his prose was good but could never be universal the way the *real* stuff was, the heterosexual generative family. My life, apparently, is not worthy of being universal; little louse of a life, swatted at. Hollinghurst won the Booker in 2005, the year I graduated high school. I sat on my school's long sloping patio, on a little island between the bay and the sea. The sea side of the beach does sound like the Greek, *Thalassa Tha-LAS-SA* as bigger waves come crashing in, the surf hitting the sand tarmac of used needles and condoms we picked up for community service. The bay, though, slaps gently, lapping cups in the wind.

It was on the bay that I pined, reading, stealing glimpses of the girl who became the Nike of Samothrace, seeing the line of beauty in the curve of her back as I read the precious imported hardback, the assignations I would never have been brave enough for, in the gardens of Kensington and Notting Hill. Seagulls stole our sandwiches and small change with abandon. I screeched at them. I can still hear Updike's prose though, too, his sentences now and then, faceted like gems. Some of them are perfect. Some of them are worth cracking an uncrackable glass vitrine in the shadows of a Dresden night.

Do you hate me now, Updike's Shade? It's okay, I'm a critic, I'm climbed into your mouth and eaten off your grey tongue. I speak your neat universals, your hard-bitten hags who used to be girls, your tired and valorous schlumps of men, I speak them for you now. I don't need my tongue, I've stolen yours.

"... with her narrow woman's mind she had cut through to the truth that would give the most hurt."

I hope so. Did you know a scalpel is a gentle touch?

My father taught me that. He cut open bodies. He, too, made the dead speak, counting their stab wounds and bullets for our Areopagus. A pathologist's daughter grows up jostling death for room in the family car, has Thanatos over for sleepovers.

To the party in the Gentlemen's Club, I wore a necklace with a silver straight razor, the blade ground down just enough that you could touch it, flip it about in your hands like a parlor trick. It could do so much less than a scalpel, know so much less, a blunt instrument like that. And yet they looked at it with fear in their eyes, the men who knew you, knew Theocritus and so many lines of Homer beaten into them in some august schoolroom. I laughed at them, stole the goddesses' flashing eyes. Hermes is, too, a thief.

Last year at Marienbad. This year in London. No one will ever stalk me through manicured gardens, cultivating mirrors and doubt. I have purloined memory, I have secreted it away, across black and white diagonal tiles, out of a safe, all the way to *Thalassa*, the bay, the sea. Full of gaping fishes, shades of books that I could succor on forever, unsuspecting, made easy and neat. I am inside that fish right now. So are you. White teeth, black gaps. A very dangerous parquet! Critics and Criticism. Fish-louses at play on a chessboard.

That's what the critical eros is too, a desire, even for the appalling but also lovely— your Heidegger, your Pound, your Brancusi birds so ovoid and sleek— to take it, clasp it, tap into the vessels of its blood and make it what you need to live, and if you're lucky, speak.

12.

I have written to Chiron, to a Chiron of my story, to ask for a copy of a lecture on Twombly. This Twombly is in the Yale University Art Gallery. It is one of the "chalkboard" paintings, that are done in a whitish wax crayon that looks as delicate and capable of quick damage as lines made of white chalk. This one is a series of rotated rectangles, the Yale one, but I'm also thinking of the scribbled loops, the uncountable lines of loops like the script of some formic queen, a bored mega-ant oozing out eggs in a cavity under the sidewalk speaking the words of a Delphic ant oracle.

Twombly was frustrated for a while, before these paintings were made, by bad sales. I am frustrated. Loops on loops on loops. Repetitions, cries in search of an answer.

I think it is true to some extent that critics are ventriloquists, that we swap out the tongue lice in our fish mouths to speak differently. There is voice for the *TLS*, a voice for the internet, and so on. I remember when I was tongueless. The end of my first semester at Yale depression took me like a black bolt, like the act of some angered god in the sky, it was so sudden and then I could hardly write or speak. For the first time in my entire life, I was often silent. I was nineteen. I waggled my stub of a tongue. I went back to my parents' house in the suburbs, back for the term, and waited for the drugs to kick in while they prodded me, with aching, unstinting tenderness, to remember to walk and sleep and eat. I mostly slept.

When I returned to university I was still broken. I could write and read, more than I could before, felt compelled to, and learned Greek in ten-hour days in an academic summer. But part of me fell away too, and I did badly in Greek and Latin, so badly I quit, and picked little holes in my skin that bled and were infected incessantly. It was then, I think, that I began my real education, put something in the mouth where the tongue should be, learned to declare savagely the quality of things and people and books.

When Chiron knew me first, and the last time we met in person, I was small for my age, and a kind of defiant Dickensian urchin with hair dyed a weak Manic Panic blue. I was angry. I wore a fisherman's coat from the Salvation Army with a whole toggle worn off, and a sweater I still have, from the Navy, with dun cloth epaulets and a thick double-knit heft.

My hair was short but fell over my eyes. In some ways I hid, hibernated inside my own little gall of blankets. But in others I had decided that I could no longer live with the unceasing happiness of my fellow students, who seemed so ignorant, in my then-ignorance, of sorrow. I don't know why, to this day, they collaborated, but I had decided the faculty would entertain me and they did. I got drunk for the first time, at the Yale Center For British Art, not realizing quite what was in mimosas. I went to Chiron's class, in which I was as any other student for a while. But the drunk day, my first drunk day, I spat back at him about acanthus in front of a lecture hall of seventy other people. He had, in my view, underestimated its importance.

Acanthus is what makes one particular outlier of the columns of the Temple of Apollo Bassae called Corinthian. It makes the more ornate of the three orders, this fern that is often such an abstraction of a fern in art that it ceases to be anything at all. In an Italian print of the 15th or 16th century, it was merely a decorative border, something that could never be *merely* when you're drunk, and actually, borders are underrated anyway. I could write a whole book about borders, the dripping rocaille acanthus surrounding the glass cases of diamonds in Dresden.

Anyway, the lecture turned into a conversation, and for reasons I still don't know, Chiron in turn decided I was worth not simply tolerating, but listening to. It was strange. I told him he was an asshole if he just wanted us to regurgitate his lectures on the midterm. I signed up, as we did then, still on paper, tacked to faculty doorways, for office hours under the name of characters from Henry James. He knew all the characters, the meaning of the crack in the Golden Bowl. I couldn't sneer at him from a safe superiority like most people I had met until then. He told me to read Benjamin. And it was he who told me to read Updike.

Sometimes you wonder if you are merely a footnote in someone else's life, when the reverse isn't true for you, as I surely am to Chiron, no matter what he says in correspondence. If he ever sees this, I'm sure he will politely demur and assure me otherwise. I think though, that a certain amount of knockdown drag out screaming fights about art in elevators later, a certain number of regrettable 2 a.m. emails, you learn something, which is not necessarily how to speak yet exactly, but that what you say matters, can wound or elevate. I didn't know then yet about the rules of things, about authorities and positions and mattering, about the difference between the Upper East and Upper West side, about proprieties of existing outside the novels I had read as a frame for everything. So in a way, I was Achillean, reckless, throwing my idiot youth at the front lines of everything, risking things I did not yet know existed to risk. And so Chiron became Chiron, and taught me, at least in this version of the story, at least before we all become Nestor and nostalgia roughs it clean. Centaurs know the secrets of medicine, of growing back tongues.

It is 11:41 p.m. on an early December Friday in London though, and Chiron hasn't emailed me back, and I am dangerously frustrated. Not bored, but sort of trapped in myself. Loop loop loop loop. The fictional screech of chalk. Loop Loop. Two handles. A *kissubion*.

In Updike's *The Centaur*, the son, Peter, is sitting in the car looking at middle America fly past his windows, and thinking too about his father, George, who is Chiron in the novel, too.

Among these images which the radio songs
rapidly brushed in for me the one blank space was
the   canvas I was so beautifully, debonairly,
and preciously   covering. I could not visualize
my work; but its featureless   radiance made the
center of everything as I carried my   father in the
tail of a comet through the expectant space of   our
singing nation.

It's one of those perfect sentences, especially that last clause,
through the expectant space of our singing nation. Except
I left America, for the Old World and its bent fig trees and
dead shepherds. Except my radiance if there is a radiance is
no longer fearless. Except I have never been a father or a son.
Except the comet ricochets across the Atlantic, in-boxes, plus
and minus 5 hours GMT. Except look, I can see the canvas, its
endless curving lines dense with expectation. Except that I feel
always the need to write this, to say something, to comment, to
run the tip of my louse's tongue onto the roof and soft palate
of the night sky, seeking out the ribbed dome underneath.

13.

It's later, but I'm still stuck in the unmoored time of weekends, in the migraine-sleep unsleep-unhuman cycle. I get a replica of the red loops in the late paintings, *Untitled 2005* and the one at the Tate, done on each of my ring fingers. I try to get Twombly's 'Cy' signature on my thumb, my biggest nail, but my manicurist has impeccable cursive and she says he writes like a child, so it's far too lovely. A colleague at the RCA has offered to kindly give me a copy of his copy of an art film that uses Twombly's paintings, one I've been trying to find screenings of but couldn't.

I am telling you all these things because they might make what is about to happen make sense. I dream about Twombly, two oddly intense almost waking dreams I'm locked into, rigid, slicked, and shivering with sweat. I have just started Genet's *The Thief's Journal* and he talks about the flowers, the convicts he has garlanded in his head, the ones in the places that smell of sperm and sweat. My sweat smells like the sweater I drifted off in, which was doused liberally in Diptyque Eau Des Sens, so I guess smell more like the metaphorical flowers. It's a no go on the sperm, obviously, but as I sit up I start cursing, knowing why the migraine has finally released. I stick my hand between my legs and it smells like an abattoir. Not that I've ever been to an abattoir. Or a French penal colony. I panic and check the sheets because I don't own the mattress and slink off to the bathroom.

The dream was the second one where I was at an august lecture. The name of the lecturer is drawn twice from life — first someone I didn't know during my PhD, an expert on Chinese art at Chicago. The second name is from my office mate's supervisor, who also doesn't work on Twombly. I am somehow not supposed to be at these lectures. This is all very strange because in real life I *give* lectures, and in any event they have never intimidated me, but in my dreams I'm so in awe of the lecturers my voice shakes when I ask questions. The second dream is in a classroom that is in a gallery, it's all dark and up a million flights of steel stairs, which isn't anywhere I can actually remember.

The lecturer has those small round glasses like Adorno, and he is gesturing at a Twombly which is somehow on the floor, and looks like a rug which is not at all a

Twombly. There are arguments that can be made about figuration and abstraction here, that Twombly is in fact a figurative painter, but this is a figure figure, I mean a person, in a way he doesn't paint. The lecturer says the man, who may be the artist, is having sex with a prostitute on Miami Beach in the scene. Which, first of all, Twombly would never paint, and second of all, he never did. I doubt he's even been to Miami Beach.

I, however, have been there, and in the dream I offer to get the lecturer the autopsy results of the woman from the '80s. I will ask the pathologist, who probably knows my father. Now, again, this isn't a Twombly, and there is no real woman, but this is something that could be true in real life. Before the regulations changed on showing autopsy photos in Florida, I used to help my father, who was incompetent at PowerPoint, put photos on slides for trials. Many of these were anonymous murders, prostitutes. The Jane Does. They died in horrible ways, in pools of blood. The woman in the painting doesn't look like this. What she looks like, a bunch of jagged lines like a spider, doesn't make much sense either, unless you're me, and have recently been looking at the levels of haemoglobin in your blood, which is my blood. Actually the fact that I'm menstruating at all at this point is weird, because I'm anaemic, my iron is really low and my haemoglobin has been mysteriously declining in lines that look like the segments of the woman's splayed limbs on the painting on the lecture-room floor in the dream. There are a number of things that can cause this and first of all, I assure you, I am not bad enough for the likely one, that I am somehow breaking my diet and eating wheat, triggering immune reactions and bleeding in the gut. Yeah, I read Genet and all that prison and conning and sweat, but I told you, I sweat a bunch in my Diptyque in my clean sheets. I'm boringly good. Except when I write critique I guess.

One possibility would be that I have a parasite, a tapeworm, but I definitely don't and the NHS would not think it was amusing were I to ask. I tell the doctor that statistically I am not going to worry that it's 'fucking cancer or something' so can he please send me my results directly and leave it to the new year. Haemoglobin carries oxygen in the blood, it is in red blood cells. It is made of Heme A and Heme B groups. It is straightforwardly from the Greek αἷμα which means blood. All over the plains of Troy etcetera, and all over Twombly. Maybe that made the dream or the period, or the migraine.

Anyhow, the lecturer captivates all of us, describing the painting-carpet he calls a Twombly, with the woman in it, the dead sex worker with the haemoglobin-chart limbs askew. And he says "No one wants queer art to be *queer* any more." Which to be clear, is my brain saying that, and yet me in the dream is somehow intimidated by his prognosticatory authority. I look at him with wide eyes and say, god help us all, that *I* want to write that. He laughs at me like I am an ambitious child. The architecture student next to me draws the painting in his notes more beautifully than it looks. I stare at it in the dream for a long time. I go to leave, my heels clanking on the dark stairs, and then I hear the lecturer yelling at some people in the front rows from a distance about *how dare they* during a lecture. They did something; what I don't know.

I wake up shivering in the puddle of my flower-sweat and hop in the shower. *Do* people not want queer art to be queer anymore? Why did dream me think that was so damn profound? Why am I so nervous in dream lectures? I use the red Twombly ring finger nail to insert a tampon.

The loops of *Untitled 2005* sear into my brain, even though arterial, fresh blood is a deeper red, and menstrual blood is browner because it is dead, actually, dead uterine lining.

Limp little heme proteins uncurling in the matrix of cotton and string. I pick up *The Thief's Journal* again.

Look I can be bad, too, Genet, I think spitefully: My body is a disconsolate abattoir! I wish, for the sake of the extended metaphor, that I actually had a tapeworm, which would also solve both the being badass and whole aetiology-of-my-anaemia problems. I sigh and put down the French prison again. I pull on large, yellow rubber gloves and dutifully clean my accumulating dishes. So much for the languorous, squalid enjoyment of my disgusting urban condition.

Critic-me, she can do that, she could rob a bank and have some sort of celebratory orgy on the soon-to-be-laundered notes, but me-me? The one that just woke up paralyzed from a dream about a Twombly lecture? She has to do things like dishes. She doesn't occupy the *expectant space of our singing nation*, make words as crimes and amorally alluring flowers. I don't know where one ends and the other begins really, but they're twined together, a rope of acanthus in an ornamental border. Maybe there aren't really two of us. Maybe I'm the horse end of the centaur and she's the man, the part with the hands and tongue. In real life, ironically, I'm actually a bit frightened of horses.

I'm the Achilles who dresses up as a dancing girl, gets hidden by his mother, avoids the war entirely. I'm her, too, and the tapeworm, and the wasp, and the fish louse, sucking blood and figs and gobbling up lines of oil paint and prose like sweat, like air, like water. *Eau Des Sens*. Water of the senses. Diptyque is just French for diptych, an altar-piece which is like a triptych, like the Hamburger-Banhof's Thyrsis of Etna, but with only two panels. It can be closed like a book. *Odyssey*, not *Iliad* this time, book 19, Penelope's Dream: there are two gates dreams pass through, one of horn, for true dreams, and one of ivory, for false ones.

The footnote in the Loeb informs us:

> The play upon the words κέρας, "horn", and κραίνω, "fulfill", and upon ελέφας, "ivory", and ελεφαίρομαι, "deceive", cannot be preserved in English

Like the bits about 'Nobody' putting out the Cyclops' eye, I swear it works in the Greek. Trust me; trust nobody. οὖτις becomes Nemo becomes Anonymous. Ivory is a type of horn anyway, isn't it? They're a set, a pair, a diptych.

14.

Here's another thing that reminds me of loops and repetitions, of Twombly's chalkboard paintings: tapeworms.

Consider the case study of the class *Cestodes*, some six thousand parasitic species. Each is made of a grappling-hook mouth, the scolex, and a long tube bit that is just repeated segments. The segments, called *proglottids*, have self-fertilized eggs on eggs in them ready to go, a certain gravid and sinister repetition. Loop loop loop. The two are close, aligned with the Twombly that lives in the Yale University Art Gallery, called simply "Untitled" and made in 1967. Tapeworms look like these faux-chalked Twombly rectangles, like *tape*, each overlapping proglottid the potential for a thousand new worms, an independent brutal unit of mass proliferation. For some scientific reason they're often stained bright pink on slides, and they even look like mid-century screen prints, some nexus of abstraction and ready-mades that also just happen to be worms.

The tapeworm segments are called *proglottids* from a bastardisation of (what else?) the Greek. It's an old one, going back to Homer, γλῶσσα, *glossa* or tongue. It's the same word as one for language itself. I am reading Rosalind Krauss's infamous essay on Twombly's chalkboard paintings, the one where she compares them to Derrida and Pollock, and in turn, graffiti. They don't look like graffiti to me, since they are so planned, so ordered, like the tapeworms and their rectangle-on-rectangle expansive infinities. They are a language somehow, yes, but I'm also still reading *The Thief's Journal*. Genet wouldn't mince words with tapeworms: it's a tongue that comes out of your ass. But does it still speak?

On Pollock, whom she compares to Twombly, Krauss in turn quotes the critic Clement Greenberg:

"He wasn't this wild heedless genius," Clem continues. "No. He wasn't that. He looked. He looked hard; and he was very sophisticated about painting." His voice trails off, as though he were remembering.

On the lice with which he was parasitized and kept company when getting by as a beggar, male prostitute, and petty thief in his youth in Spain, Genet writes:

"The lice inhabited us. They imparted in our clothes an animation, a presence, which, when they had gone, left our garments lifeless. We liked to know—and feel—that the translucent bugs were swarming... Having become useful for the knowledge of our

> *decline as jewels, for the knowledge of what is called triumph,*
> *the lice were precious."*

Precious disgusting things; when they extract them out of people tapeworms are sometimes so long, whole feet or meters long, that sometimes they wind their gelid bodies, those sacs of egg masses, around a nearby stick. Incidentally, I am not reading Genet in the original French, you can tell. Translators, tongue-to-tongue, *glossa-to-glossa*, have to be careful, forming a language in between, like Greenberg thinks Pollock was, and maybe Twombly was too. And critics? We're the lice or maybe also the worms, or the fish-louse tongues, but whatever the case we have to be undetectable enough to sneak in under the immunological/itch-sense radar. Hardly thieves or confidence men, maybe beggars, hardly some *wild heedless genius*, the one we all wish we were when we're in the dark gut of the thing, roiling, latched in, and sucking-supping thick intestinal blood with the hooks where our mouths should be.

I like the idea of the tapeworm's *scolex* because it is frightening, because if critics can in some way be tapeworms, clinging in the guts of authors and poems and tracts and paintings, then I have a scolex too. One of my bosses told me yesterday that if I wanted him to promote me for jobs in the academy, it was not sufficient to be brilliant or good, that in fact, though he did not say this, there was no *wild heedless genius*, no words I could make. I was supposed to be NICE instead. Yes, a nice little worm, polite and forgiving, sweet, and certainly not siphoning off blood or shit until my subject material expired, some orgiastic last gasp of ekphrasis into the night. This command to niceness, of course instead, made me want to be disgusting, untouchable, speaking dark argots in corners slick with grime. Get my scolex out, lob it into the head of a Lapith, or maybe a Centaur, because whose side is barbarism on again anyway? Mine, maybe, in the arena, or the flat-not-flat tape-rectangle segment of a single Parthenon metope. And Genet, Genet, he knew this already, from his lice, who are *knowledge of our decline as jewels, for the knowledge of what is called triumph*. There is a kind of triumph in grossness, in parasitism as critical mode, that feels not nice, and good about it.

Practical question: Does Chiron get horse parasites or human ones, or both? Or neither? Updike is far too dignified to tell me this, his Chiron gets hit by an arrow and suspects cancer, forlorn in Ohio with car problems in the snow. Genet would definitely tell me, though, and then fuck him after for good measure. Chiron, not Updike, though I suppose, with Genet, all things are possible.

I grow prolix and long with sacs full of eggs, made from the nutrient slop of everything I see and hear and read. I wag my body, my segments, and it is a tongue and these are its words, asshole words I have stolen like a petty thief, words I cherish because they are not agreeable, but somehow wretched and ready to disseminate and breed.

15.

Criticism isn't theft, in Genet's way or any way really, but then again neither is parasitism. The wasp burrows into the unspent flower of the fig tree with the imperative to live. The fish louse takes the place of the tongue of the fish to survive. The tapeworm attaches to the wall of the gut for the same reason. Taste can be cultivated, a sort of *eros* of wanting certain things, but behind taste is the throbbing want that is perhaps closest to the parasitic, Darwinian imperative. "We tell ourselves stories in order to live" is the kind of thing that ends up on inspirational posters for children's English classrooms. Maybe we do, but if we're critics, we feed on art not to live, but to feel the heady rush at the apex of the senses. This not-exactly-nice thing, this assignation of sorts; I read and look, greedy for it.

So it is like Genet's theft in that way, in that it is an art, learned through hard apprenticeship and desire. The desire in theft in Genet that comes out of an excess of something (and not a necessity) is where it feels most like criticism, sex, or both.

Remember the jewel thieves in Dresden, the ones who might have been last year at Marienbad. Actually they're not the parasites here. Again, the theft was likely commissioned. Nor is the person who wanted the state jewels of Saxony all to themselves— and crucially to no one else — when an object is custom- swiped in robbery like a parasite.

The ultimate acquirer of the stolen diamonds isn't like the thieves, if they are Genet's thieves, or the critics, who do a thing in the world and then leave it there. If I am greedy for say, a novel, or Bruegel's Fall of Icarus, or the piano sonatas of the Younger of the Scarlattis, I don't take it from the world. Or I do, a version of it, and put it in my Simoneidean memory house which is perhaps also a private brothel. But the Bruegel is still there, the Scarlatti, the novel, to seduce other people, other critics. Parasites want their hosts to live so they can spread. Critics can be parasites because they don't secret away the diamonds, break the vitrines of the public museum.

Tapeworms have innate in their proglottids the capacity to make an exponentially greater number of more tapeworms. Essays make essays this way, maybe with footnotes, and reviews make viewers who are in a sense, themselves critics. When I love someone, a person, my Nike of Samothrace, I am a jealous creature. I want no one else to have her, to be loved in a singular and only return. This is not how I love that about which I write, the things with which I want to infect others, to make them also love, or lust, a review bursting like a cloud of *psenes* from a gall. They sting you and you want it, whatever I just wrote about; the Twombly or the Genet. Maybe even the diamonds of Saxony. Have you bought a copy of *The Centaur* already? I have infected you too.

I have kissed you with another's usurped kiss of the mouth. This is criticism too, me seducing you on behalf of some dead thing bound in folio. We have a tryst when you read this. Open even the most stolid of review pages, of a literary magazine or a Sunday broadsheet, and I contaminate you with my desire. The newsprint on your fingers is like the smear of lipstick I could leave on your cheek. Afterward you see it and wonder what prompted you to this, if my gentle bite still marks the soft nape of your neck.

There is a proglottid there now, just as say, Sontag, has left one in me. We all infect each other.

This argot, of contagion, of closeness, of rooms with chess-board floors and glass walled displays of implacable treasures, is Genet's argot of thieves, but it is also the argot of the city, a certain kind of crowded city where people are formed into themselves as if by a greater topographical will. When I picture this city I see a 17th century print by a man named Wenceslaus Hollar. He was an immigrant to London, but this print is the Holy Land, part of an imagined set of plans, elevations, and finally this realization, of the Temple of Jerusalem. He wants to establish the baroque proportions of the Temple's façade, but it is so wildly dense, folded back onto itself, that it feels like a puzzle or a Borgesian trick. It is squares on squares, an endless fractal-like array that plunks rhythmically until it hits a gaping cavernous ooze at the size of the complex.

The architecture of this Jerusalem is that of a city of gods, but also thieves. It is simultaneously distant, as we see it from a bird's eye view in the plan, but still, you can hear thwack thwack repeats the façade in rhythms in each nested square. Thwack thwack thwack, loop loop loop; Twombly's chalkboards ring here too. Not graffiti but a floor plan, a number of columns that approaches the uncountable, or the countable only to a god. Proglottids gravid with stacked eggs, extending one after the other after the other after the other until they almost exceed the human scale. Perhaps this is a holy place because it is a limit of knowing, a limit of what it is possible to desire, and therefore, to critique.

PART 2

I have conversed with the spiritual Sun. I saw him on Primrose Hill
—Blake

The following are fit topics for conversation for men reclining on a soft couch by the fire in the winter season, when after a meal they are drinking sweet wine and eating a little pulse: Who are you, and what is your family? What is your age, my friend? How old were you when the Medes invaded this land?
—Xenophanes, Fragments 17

1.

I'm on Primrose Hill, walking without my heart rate shooting up for the first time in days, and I don't have a spiritual sun. The early days of the pandemic has us all invoking the etymology of quarantine: quaranta, Venice, ships for forty days, ships with little stick oars in Twombly not getting anywhere near Lepanto, thanks, but that doesn't even scare me — considering the futility of the little stick oars against the raging sea. It's just my broken immune system acting up again, set to kill, making my face a flaming constellation and my irregular adrenaline surges like I've got Priam by the hair and I'm about to behead him on his own altar. I rage. I rage at the world and myself and the angry emeritus professor across an ocean who didn't like my piece in a book review, and so assumed it was I, the little petulant girl, who must have some animus. Not I, the critic, the one who could eviscerate arguments or Myrmidons, not I who *noticed his intellectual failure*.

Arrow to tendon on the back of the ankle, the bowstring snaps, and the barbed tip lands. I can do this trick too, sons of Peleus, I can stand on the field with you and bristle.

And so the petty email eats at me. I imagine myself eating him, the hapless professor, literally tearing apart the steaming guts of his corpse like a predatory beast. I look up from the coiled offal and bare my teeth at you. I don't want to be nice, and when a girl on an online dating platform tells me I should reframe my intelligence, so as not to scare people, I go molten. You just want me to be *nice* so you don't have to be scared of me. Of *us*. Of all the angry creatures that can crawl out of lexica and dusty shelves with obsidian pebbles spitting from their mouths when they speak. I tell her this: *someday I want to be fucking terrifying*. I want to die alone with snakes for eyes. Maybe they will send me under the city like the Furies, who niced up to the "Eumenides" in the end anyway. Kindly Ones is what Eumenides means in English. Yeah, right—have you seen a Fury lately? They speak my kind of Greek.

In a Homeric fashion I wanted to drag the petty email man's body around the corpse of my humanities, the one I am always too late for. No jobs, just ghosts. Nothing left in the embers, nothing still stirring, just cold coal, and the sheets of rain. I will shear my hair and cast it on a pyre for the bitterness of the thing I love, or that I once loved, if it's gone already. There will be funeral games, the prizes will be cortisol, prostiglandins, tryptases, histamines, all rearing to go like I've got half the Trojan army marshaling on my right eyelid, which now looks like I've been punched. I usually hate reading the sack of Troy. I hate that the Romans salted the earth of Carthaginian fields after the third Punic war. I hate cruelty. I hate in the mirror the red spot flares, hives down each of my cheeks all Achillean red.

Have you seen the Achilles from *Fifty Days At Iliam*, the Twombly Achilles? It's a big red mountain of an A, which critics who are other critics and not me, are fond of calling a phallus. I want to look these old men who hate me in the eyes and say "Be afraid. Die angry". I want to salt their fields and take their wives and children, and sear their cities of the mind seven burn layers into some Schliemann-sucked field. Only the oak will be left standing, the one in the middle of the plain. At this moment, I have taken from the texts the entirely wrong and desperate lesson. I succour in it nastily.

There are people who think the Greeks, and particular Homer, are smooth and talk in voices for drawing rooms, or for oratoria, but not this voice, which is to say mine and high and shrill. You call us the Eumenides because you are afraid to find us still under your own cities, wandering in the night. You are afraid of me as I am; of the Greeks as they are, angry and various, and Homer rocking away blind in the dark which does not admit the image of you, o tame thing who has forgotten all its old names and hunts them in echoes of Shakespeare as if this were a mirror, as if a mirror is not an instant a thousand spike shard projectiles looking at your face.

By contrast, it was a calm evening and there was an early moon on the Hill, round and perfect like a Magritte. The pinkish skies and the stripped winter branches reminded me particularly of "The Banquet", the way the gloaming always feels pregnant with things about to happen. He does this with a color field alone, Magritte, the orange round circle of the declining sun. This is the space where the glass of the mirror used to be, hanging in a hallway where none of us can exactly remember the story of the film, that nonetheless feels like story indeed. The glowing ember of this sun is inside a clutch of darkening trees, a calm stone wall just sitting quietly. My anger is perhaps receding now, though still too dangerous for anything but a long steel poker in a fireplace, turning the ashes of the sky.

Blake loves the sun on Primrose Hill, the exalting soul of it in midday, not this halfway-to-night-burnt-sun. I have always been a night creature, a 3 a. m. cryptid, a Fury with an inverse sleep schedule. I like walking in the dark in the City when the office buildings are all lit up and empty, imagining sneaking into them, into their lives. I walk around Wren and Hawksmoor and Jones churches not far from the Thames. I too would have been afraid of this in the past, I think, but now they should be afraid of me, whoever they are, in the cool breathing of baroque stone and lacquered wood, the insouciant sheen of modern glass edifices with swipe-ins, as if this renders them somehow impenetrable. We are none of us impenetrable. I don't converse with the moon, but we do regard each other warily.

When two or more male fig wasps are trapped inside a fig with only one female, there is a kind of battle royale to the death. If there are truly only two, two especially of the species who have evolved rhinoceros-like armor for the entire 36 hours of their brief lives, they go mano-y-mano, Achilles on Hector, chasing against the long edge of the wall—the wall at Troy, deceptively calm like the stone of Magritte. They choose *kleos* and dying young. They do not run away disguised as dancing girls. There is no fig wasp Nestor. Anyway, the winner gets to mate and then die anyway. It's still, for the parasites, as usual, the end of the world. It's always the end of the world when your existence is basically mate quickly and die. It's the end of the world again here now too, all plague and apocalypse, and stuck in our flats soon like we'll be rolled up inside fig galls to fight it out. I'll be fine. I do my best work in the dark. It's bloody there.

I look at my corticosteroid translucent skin, and trace my capillaries like subterranean creeks. I try to see the other side of myself that remains, that wept so many times for Priam, for the sack of the city and any city, for Cassandra, for Achilles too even, for the idea of the war. I try and try but right now, when I should feel the empathy in fragility, I feel only the obverse. The already dead are never afraid to die. The angry male fig wasps cannot, evolutionarily, stop to be afraid of anything. I trust no one, and envy all of history selfishly. They had so much *time*.

I stay here in London, here in Twombly's crimson heap of burning Achilles painting, because I can't stop, because no fig-wasp just turns around and says "nevermind, actually," and walks out of the fig. Because I took the wrong lesson from Homer and chose anger and revenge and death and glory a long time ago already, probably. Because I am already too late, it is already dusk. The world is sick and on fire and I'm bent under a duvet, staring at the red-slopped vengeance of Achilles, the canvas with the lines like penciled in spears. The red on top looks like fresh arterial blood, like it's not even set yet, when it would be brownish and clotted. Perhaps Twombly probably would just be another old man who thought I was unworthy of thinking this analogy. He can be afraid from the grave, stay dead angry then. Haven't I just plucked the eye-balls out of his corpse and put them in my sockets just now? I'm Doctor Coppelius. I am already dead and here dancing a light waltz in a toyshop tutu, reanimate and constitutionally incapable of being afraid.

All Twombly As look like the letter delta in Greek, actu-ally. Alphas into deltas—belated alphabets, even, are the lots we've been given here, we evening children. The Magritte painting glows background blue-white now on my screen as I shut it for bed. It is exhausting being a Fury. It is impossi-ble to burn both so long, or so brightly, with rage. It will stay dormant here, curled into the nexus of my desire, coming up occasionally to run hot in my veins. Troy was sacked so long ago. The fields are salted everywhere already. All the battles royale are decided. The shields are in museums and poems and novels. Maybe I was born too late for rage, but I hope I am not Peleus's son in other ways, either. How do you look at the plain, the beach, the walls of the city, the oak trees and the cauldrons on the tripods over small fires—how do you look at it all and live with the fact that you are always *after*? Always, somehow, about to break into tenderness and despair?

All the people stay at least two meters apart in the park. No one is coughing yet. I lay in oat crackers, rice, and a desire to savage something; to rip apart the old world again, since I will never know what it is to live in it. To destroy, to end things instead of make them, is suddenly appealing, almost tacitly good. I feel feral, like a raging Lapith, hurtling out of white marble, leg askew where the stone has been broken.

2.

I have burnt through my rage. Temporarily, I have lapsed from terrifying into a kind of quiet, bated breath. The virus is here and we are self-isolating, which means life almost as usual for those of us who write and isolate anyway, who isolate in crowds and on streets because you can't be a flâneur if you don't anyhow, cultivate a kind of always being alone that is. I arrange to give a lecture online on plague objects because my reflex is always to perform, dazzle. Isn't this the duty of the public intellectual after all, to make you sad if we die suddenly, to make our criticism feel somehow necessary to anyone besides ourselves? The question of necessity looms. Viruses aren't parasites in the sense that they don't always meet the definition of being alive, and in that they parasitize the replication mechanisms of our cells as they run through our bodies, not the larger corpora.

They go through hosts quickly, a kiss and kill, or a kiss and breathlessness. Italy, we hear, does not have enough respirators. They are on war triage. If it was France I could maybe count on my barely-there credit, emerging *belles lettres* maybe, and parasitize my way to a breathing apparatus if I am dying. Here in Britain though, I think I have no more claim to essentialness than anyone else, which feels right. We are leveled in our humanity before death like a Holbein print, or a danse macabre in manuscript. We are all equal before nothing. We hoard toilet paper. Everything is shut up. It is quiet and I can hear birds outside my city windows. I have already read Defoe again. I'm circling around Serres, and Homer. When you are alone you circle and circle more lazily, commit less to deciding to write.

I could circle myself forever or at least for a few weeks. I think about how I am beginning to live in necropolitics, how I and my city are just waiting to be dead in these early days. Since I mostly feed off dead things anyway, the art and the books, maybe I am suited for our new Necropolis. I'm a scavenger now. Many parasites are. I hope the city still has something to scavenge, if once we're shut up for good I can take a hoarded protein bar and walk across the Millennium Bridge and stand in front of the closed doors of the Tate Modern, looking at Wren steeples that went up after the last great plague. Scraps of skyline, of memory, of urbanities which necessitate also, the risk of quick spread of disease. Is to feed off this, as I am writing now, to look at the arts and things of death, an ignoble parasitism especially? A necrophilia?

Many upper class Romans had formal mosaics designed to look like table scraps. They're expensive scraps, oyster shells and birds stuffed in other birds and the *trompe l'oeil* looks like the *Satyricon* feels. Late. For dinner. For Empire. This motif is called, in Greek, *asarotos oikos*, unswept floor, and the one Hadrian made is in the Vatican. There are no people allowed there now, in the Vatican and on the mosaic of table scraps, just police, and a few harried priests. At 8 p. m. they are ringing all the bells on the Trastevere, they tell us, singing songs in quarantine from balconies and windows. In a year this will be poignant, in five nostalgic, and ten we will probably forget. The floors mostly do get swept. The dead are already dying.

Margeurite Yourcenar's Hadrian, as the real one did in less literary and novelistically styled evidence, spent a lifetime mourning the death of his lover Antinous. Statues of him litter the Mediterranean, a beautiful slip of a boy turned posthumously and obligatorily, almost, into a cultic god. He is a singular table scrap or maybe a whole table, a finely fluted chair. In the midst of this, in life and death, I'm still the creature that cares about things like later good emperors and their mosaic floors. I need the populated world of the daytime city, it makes my inlaid oysters, but to be a parasite alone and together at once, the byproduct of the internet, means it's never between just me and the scraps of the dead, tiled and otherwise. Everything is always already historicized into tesserae and laid out. What is there to do but look and look?

Antinous too became a cast-off thing, and if we are to believe he cast himself into the Nile. Perhaps the crocodiles worried off his arms and the fish his eyes. I stare at his marbles, the bust of him next to Hadrian's at the British Museum, fingering with my eyes his pectorals, their taut lines. The deadest prettiest queer boy in the whole world. We all claim him, decadent needy maggots slipping off the marble from Carrara of that collarbone, so prominent, so delicately arched— that long ago dissolved into the sea. It is so much easier to be dissolved than an Antinous, so entirely remembered.

If I ever love a girl the way I love the one who was the Nike of Samothrace, I promise I won't turn her into a God, with hymns and temples and paratext. I'm selfish about my own beauties, don't want them carved out for everyone to see, or perhaps I just don't want to subject them to all those eyes. Because I am a historian and a critic, this makes me a wild and contrarian hypocrite. Everyone's dead lovers are mine to latch on to. If I ever love again I don't know if I could bear it, sharing a lover with the eyes and pages of the world. Or maybe my real lovers are all the eyes and all the pages and all the tesserae that make table scraps permanent and if one could aspire to be a table scrap, would that be such a bad thing?

If I meet her now, I won't know. I'm too busy, as everyone is, estimating the contents of my fridge-freezer, counting the dead, living on the fat of my summers, their hazy reminiscences, typing and typing as if that somehow girds me into wasp or maggot, when wasps and maggots are real and present dangers for the corpse. When we stop counting the corpses later, this will feel strange, but it's not later yet, or rather, it's already too late.

I was born too late for the glimmering capitals. I was after the Doric, Ionic, Corinthian; after the Brutalist walls the shape of optimisms piled up. If the Necropolis will have me, I will sing to it, licking the salt off its long empty floors, the memories of memories of banquets. My taste is for stone, for precariously perched architraves that fall into picturesque

Grand Tour ruins, but anything will do, this flat even. If you are reading this to my particular ruin, if it has somehow survived, say hello to it for me. I hope it is a good one. I hope the vines are splitting apart the seams of the old brick and the plane trees are shading you in the hot London summer; the plane trees that in their Tradescantian hybridity, shed their catkins for scavengers, litter the ground with spiked, round pods. Hold one in your hand and feel the insistently small push of the end of each spine, one after the other, alive alive alive. Belated belated belated.

In the overgrowth, nothing will ever again be as white as the housepaint on an early Twombly. Look somewhere else for your grief, for your need, for your absence. Dig up my corpse, this very page of it, and eat it; the wasp dissolved in the fig in the ground that grew once into a tree. Kiss my bones with your eyes as I have done, greedy in this moment of caesura, kissed hotly spines of bound antiquities.

3.

The translator of Serres warns us: Parasite acquires an additional meaning in French, noise, like the static on the radio or the old snow on a TV screen. Actually there isn't much noise in the world now, just buffering, buffering as we're all trapped inside on the internet. Everything's a signal.

But anyhow yes this word, which is just *parasite* like in English but with the additional carried meaning, is in the opening note to Serres' writing in *Parasite*, a book I should have read, admittedly, well before starting to write this one. But I'm on Serres tonight and not Thoreau, because I threw Thoreau against the wall in a fit of rage, because Thoreau isn't *enough* right now, and wasn't really, ever. The danger of things being not enough grows with every day inside.

I look up Michel Serres. Member of Académie Française, of course, École normale supérieure, son of a bargeman ascended to French Intellectual Godhead. I wish I could someday aspire to this Godhead, by the way, which seems to entitle you to write anything you want or touch across the span of the humanities, to just be at play and have the world shrug and say "ah but he is an intellectual". Like Serres who, just before he died, apparently said to Hans Ulrich Obrist (whose currency seems to at least partly depend on getting important people to say interesting things like this): "I think that out of this place of no law that is the Internet there will soon emerge a new law, completely different from that which organized our old metric space."

***

The whole world is so new now, there will surely be a spate of essays like this one, about The Before and After, or there will be no After and there will still be essays anyway. I think of a fragment of Xenophanes I accidentally heard recited by an Iranian poet on exile, on Radio 3 at 4 a.m. once, but can only find the poor Victorian translation:

> The following are fit topics for conversation for men reclin-ing on a soft couch by the fire in the winter season, when after a meal they are drinking sweet wine and eating a little pulse: Who are you, and what is your family? What is your age, my friend? How old were you when the Medes invaded this land? —
> Xenophanes, Fragments 17

Xenophanes was pre-Socratic, old-old to us, and yet already looking forward to a kind of past nostalgia, time in a bou-strophedon origami, folding back on itself like when an ox, which is of course a Greek ox, plows a field in turning lines. The future of the past which is still a past to us, in this future. A better loose translation would be:

> The following are suitable topics for conversing, for
> men reclining on soft couches,
> by the fire in winter,
>
> full after a meal they are drinking sweet wine and
> eating a bit of chickpea:
>
> Who are you, and what is your family? What is
> your age, my friend?
> How old were you when the Mede came?

When the Mede came — that is, the Persian Wars. The Mede is the stock Athenian word for Other sometimes. In Iran, in Persia, the death toll for the virus is currently very high. American sanctions are making it worse. We won't say when the Mede came, will we? We are the Mede too. We'll say, when the isolation began, when the virus came, how old were your parents? And you? Your family? We'll look at this divot of history like the ox looks back over the plow, lines and lines furrowed for spring planting. The Athenian Fever in Pericles' time, hundreds of years after this poem was already old, was called "Λοιμός των Αθηνών"— that is to say, *of Athens*. It killed Pericles, but not Thucydides, who tells us about it. It was typhoid fever or maybe haemorrhagic of some kind, we don't know for certain, we can just count the increase in bodies inside the war-barricaded walls, piled in mass graves. Loop loop loop; a plague pit is also a stacked repetition.

Our Old Metric Space, that's the past past, but we are also the past to someone's future, the one that turns when the ox does with the line of the plow, the line that will become seeded with heavy heads of barley or wheat that come up in the fall. I am too late for the Old Law, for the old spaces it entangled, but am I too early yet, for the new one? Delineations of before and after do not exist yet. It is always just becoming evening, an eternal Magritte.

I hang the cat-eared pink headphones from a stick-on hook on the wall, the makeshift office wall that now resides behind my table. I take the Serres and the Bosch catalog to read in bed, or just run my hands over. I have forgotten when to wake, and sleep. Even at Iliam they slept, after the fires under the cauldrons burnt out and everyone went to his tent, except maybe Odysseus, sneaking out in the night; killing, raiding softly.

Into the night then, I email Chiron. The age of centaurs perhaps has passed with the age of men. But here we are, sending flashes in cables buried deep under the Atlantic, like a thunderbolt from Zeus' sky, for all we know of its enchantment, its true mechanisms. I send him the Xenophanes.

Is it the duty of the critic, like the historian, to always be looking back? Which one looks at portents, asks the augurs about the futures promised in the sky? Who plows the field, lays down the contour of the lines in the wagon's reins? Who knows and wants to know, and who has to?

I recline into my duvet. I take a little bite of an apple, already going brown. How old were you when the Mede came?

4.

I have taken to walking further out in the small hours, and it is 3:30 a. m. on Primrose Hill. I am listening to a Sufjan Stevens album now, a new suite of lushly dark electronica. There are no humans in the night anymore. I see two russet foxes, bushy tailed and surprised by my presence as I am. One night I sprinted ahead of the park closure van to get into Regent's Park in the dark, and lurk there along the back of the zoo. I visited the two Bactrian camels. You can tell they are Bactrian because they have two humps like the letter "B", a child's mnemonic. They are shaggy and placid. Bactria, it should be noted, did not go well for the campaigns of Alexander. But these two made me suddenly joyous and I ran in zigzags across the unused soccer pitches, filling my lungs with clean cold air that doesn't taste like London. Then, I was just as soon crushed, damp with sadness.

Tonight the foxes and I scavenge. Maybe criticism will survive after this, scavenging on the ruins of what's left. Is that really so grim? I am always telling my students that like Benjamin, I find the ruin fertile. It makes things, art and pleasure. I told you to give mine kisses, after all. *Bisou, bisou, bisou* on some crumpled acanthine pillar eroded by time.

***

The album I am listening to is called *Aporia*. απορια the moment in a philosophical discourse when you all hit the wall, an impasse that's flat up against meaning you can't quite grab yet. It's a dead end that is also a ruin, that is also productive in that strange way ruins are. I feel that in the velveteen embrace of the slight fog, in how it makes the night darker. I stick the ends of my fingertips out of the top of my fingerless gloves, and feel them go a little raw as I descend from the view of the skyline at the Hill's summit. I wave my hands like unsteady oars, like Twombly's little boats, rocking toward Lepanto. Or rocking from Lepanto, in the bloody grey of the sea.

The Lepanto series was done in 2001. The boats look like childish stick figures but there's no *wild heedless genius* in that. It's careful genius, diagrammatic, a boat stripped down to its most essential: a keeled form and three stick-like arms to row with. The seas in the Lepanto paintings are dappled with smacks of bright red and yellow. The Battle of Lepanto in 1571 was when the Holy Roman Empire scored a decisive victory against the Ottomans, and there are the normal triumphal paintings about that, but I don't see that here, and I don't think Twombly was some simple triumphant. He had a house in Gaeta, for the views of the sea. Anyway, Lepanto is the Italian medieval name for a Greek town that in Thucydides functions as a turning point in the Peloponnesian War. Ναύπακτος, the shipyard where fleet of the Heracleidae sprung. Not child's play at all, those sharp-prowed boats, the ones black with pitch. Philip, the king of Macedon, and Alexander's father, gave the city to the Aetolians.

I don't hear much about Nafpaktos, in modern Greece, since the islands are closed to visitors. I check a Reuters article, to see if the virus is marching to Rome, to Gaeta, to the house by the sea where you can go and see gardens and little sailing ships, where I will go when this is over, I tell myself like an incantation. The article reads:

> So far there have been 74 deaths in Campania, the worst affected southern region. The central region of Lazio, around the capital Rome, has registered 95 fatalities.
>
> The total number of confirmed cases in Italy rose to 74,386 from a previous 69,176, the Civil Protection Agency said.

Lepanto VIII has just the vertical keels of the boats in lines carefully made in red oil crayon. Most of the canvas is covered by violent splats of yellow and red, that run down like blood or a current. The first panel of the series is just black on white, the keels and oars and maybe even sails undamaged as they set out. Perhaps we are on panel II or III, when Twombly makes the canvas a falsely soothing turquoise, like a suburban swimming pool in the light, where only tiny red and yellow streaks flare up like flames.

The world holds its breath at the shipyard, the little oars, my arms flung out running down the hill in the cold with my fingertips splayed. I was too late, but now all I do is wait and wait, because it is too early yet, for panel XI, when some of the ships are just echoes of ships printed in red and the yellow is fading and all that's left are husks of things. But we're not there yet. 95 dead in Lazio. It is only just the beginning of quarantine in London.

Aporia in the small hours is where I feel it most, both the belatedness and the sense of waiting. I feel up against it, wanting to want something, to break into knowing and desire again, but I just watch. The camels eat their hay and sleep in front of a Brutalist building that also has humps. The foxes and I dodge each other warily.

The boustrophedon lines of a field go back and forth and turn at the ends, but I've never seen oxen really do this, and I've never sat on a wagon. There is no sun, real or spiritual, for hours yet on Primrose Hill. I am a worm and I do not think I yet forgive the plow.

I was thirty-three when the Mede came.

5.

At 4:13 a. m., several days later, I am on the hill when I see the two foxes again. We are less wary now. I can tell one from the other by the white tip of her tail. I have never been so alone in a city before. I stand on the top of Primrose Hill and it's like I'm inside the flesh of a fig. London's buildings are only half lit up, seen through the teeth of the fish whose tongue I've stolen. I am listening to Tallis and Taverner. I look at the fox with the white tail and she looks back at me, as if we should offer each other some benediction. Some people find faith during plagues. I found Taverner and Tallis and Byrd again, the *Missa Corona Spinea*, which is *no*, not about the coronavirus at all, it's the Latin word for crown and quite frequent, it's for the Crown of Thorns on the head of Christ during the crucifixion. The god which does not apply to me, or the fox. I look and she looks until our gaze breaks and I think, should

I have gotten on my knees? I laugh quietly.

It feels absurd, as if there is no space here to sacralize, as if we are stripped of that for all our rituals and masks. It's not a mitzvah if you tell anyone by the way, I say to myself, as if this had some Talmudic weight, in my internal debate as to whether to leave the foxes some extra sausages. I should point out, failed Jew that I am, that they are pork sausages, and very good with maple.

The virus looks like you spun the crown of thorns around a circle, forming a sphere with points extruding from it. This is what the catkins of the London plane trees look like too, still hanging now from the branches. Incidentally, when someone is crucified they die, if not first of blood loss, from asphyxiation. The feet cannot quite rest when nailed and the victim cannot move the ribcage to draw breath. If you die of coronavirus, your lungs fill with fluid and cytokines and even if you are on a ventilator, you sometimes asphyxiate too. Sleepovers with Thanatos— remember? This is what you whisper to yourself in your makeshift tent made out of your parents' sheets: the various ways of expiration. This is the *Iliad*, the oncoming slaughter of all the names in Book II, as if one crucifixion tallies up really, but here in the dark, with *Missa Corona Spinea*, it's not the death that matters paradoxically, but the now-sacred bloody crown, the relic. You can hear the spines in the stems of the long, clear notes.

The relic of the crown of thorns was received by Saint Louis IX from Baldwin II. It was one of the things they needed to consecrate Notre Dame when it was first built. During the recent fire at Notre Dame, the firefighters risked their lives to bring it out, because it is the relic that activates the cathedral, because without it the cathedral's not a conduit to anything, not powered up. A relic is a kind of sacral battery, AA for the appropriate slot. The crown is in a circular reliquary of pure crystal wound with nineteenth century gilt, and blue, lapis blue, French crests appended at the axes. The boys' choir singing Taverner shoots soprano untraced into the vaulting of the sky. I run across the bridge back to my one small room, not yet an everywhere, for all my attempts. Between approximately 3:45 and 5:15 a. m. I feel most alive. Other times it is like I am behind rock crystal, muffled, but more fragile and luminous than glass, a statue of Antinuous still stuck in the cloudy water of the Nile.

Oh, and now that I am thinking clearly, in the crispness of new air, I must disabuse you about the Twombly, the Lepanto panels. The way they were meant to be hung, and hence the numbers, at Museum Brandhorst in Munich, means that they flash in strange order between whole ships, minor flares, and yellow red splots. There are blown out coronas of boats where boats used to be in various post-Homeric blood feuds, scarred and re-erased into the paint. Actually, maybe Twombly wasn't just thinking of Lepanto in its classical time, or the Ottomans, but really all the times it sparked up in between and after. His blue of the sea is not wine-dark but an aquamarine I remember from Biscayne Bay in Miami, where my school was on an island, a beach. Shallow, calm water, like in a harbor or where you walk halfway in before you bob up and swim.

Anyway, the Lepanto sequence isn't linear: it's *ship- ships-battle-battle-ships*, as if the memories are flashing inward unwilled, like when you close your eyes with a headache and there are spindly invasions and patches of light, red against your capillaries. It's visual PTSD. It's social memory inscribed in paint. Or maybe it's PTSD for battles you never fought or will fight. If you parasitize properly, throw yourself into it, you might emerge a changed thing. If I trap a catkin in a crystal reliquary before they all open and cast their flurry of pollen to the wind in spring, maybe someday it will activate when you behold it, or touch it with your eyes. It will turn wherever you are, that reader-future you, into a battlefield or a cathedral, all the treble soaring points of impossible masses. If we make a relic of the now they can consecrate chaplets in the ruins with it, scattered across the grounds of our cities like table leavings. They, too, will write how it moved them, how it moves *us* to suffer at a distance: looking from the white-walled gallery at every battle at Lepanto, every dead son of every foreign god, foxes.

PART 3

1.

.

I am forgetting how to be human. Case study: time. It no longer exists in a comforting, round volvelle that is raised slightly from the vellum of the page. I no longer go round it in comforting cycles, night and day. Between Good Friday and Easter Sunday, again neither do I find faith in any god, nor a sleep schedule. The Prime Minister goes into hospital but does not die. I write things pinned to gifs, bright looping images that go on forever and also only for an instant. I read Borges fitfully. Is this what it means to wrap my tongue around the language of the Coming World, the After? Does it have fricatives and clicks or glottal stops? I read Rilke in neon. Everything flares out as if unto an unseen lens. Everything is metropolitan, dense, peopled, but also somehow absent, solitary, and alone. The skyline of London is dotted with lights of buildings I may not see for months, a year even. I remember when I went up the Shard last, I remember staring down at all the spires of the Wren churches arrayed out in the hot summer. I want so much to be disaffected in public rather than in private, in the cold glare of some sticky club, leaving, always leaving under the blinking sign.

There is no neon in Twombly, really, except the white. The white has a kind of iterative brightness that suggests it is not a creamy, stuccoed friendly white, but a spraycan-shocker bloodshot-eyes white. It is somehow Cycladic, like the islands in the Aegean, monumental and timeless. It is also somehow a fitful, modern, efficient, Taylorised color, like a generic industrial production line; because white is all the other colors in the spectrum at once.

If we are going to keep doing this criticism thing, I think to myself, the new language better come in fast and arterial, bloom into our thoracic selves, into the little nidus cubby-nests of flats scattered around the globe. I remember longing to be cozy once, wrapped, nested up. Now I just want to be exposed. There is no thrill to writing about dead art for a dead world in a dead city. The Necropolis is never moved and we are becoming the Necropolis, all of us, until something manages to mean again, I mean *mean* in a real way that death means, or the awareness of it, brevity, a kind of *mono no aware* or *et in Arcadia ego*, but for now, for the blue glowing screens of individual and accidental monasticisms.

We just say "the virus" now, not even Covid or Covid-19, because it is evident. The concept of vaccination is bandied about with longing. We will all spend the summer wasting, a line from a song of a Scottish band I loved from the late '90s, when spending the summer wasting was wasting time and not time wasting you, eating away at the hours. Tomorrow is yesterday is last week again. I skim everything and latch on to nothing. A parasite that fails to feel or feed will die.

Rilke is moved by a torso, a severed torso of an Apollo from the peak of Athenian Greece. Maybe he saw it at the Glyptothek in Munich. He writes it a poem, a poem that I have always considered both extremely gay and extremely trite. I have wanted to understand Rilke and failed a number of times, lacking the sort of frustration of feeling, or of words for experience, that I know now.

You must change your life. *Du mußt dein Leben ändern.*

Well, obviously, obviously. I always thought this last line of a poem was plonking, overmuch, over-arty, over-felt, but who am I to over-anything from a one bedroom I haven't left in days? I thought there were two Sundays, as in today was Sunday but also yesterday by accident. *Du mußt dein Leben ändern*, Rilke practically shouts at me, an unseen god. I see these words in every circling gif image of signs about feelings in teenagers' rooms, in the adolescent loneliness of cityscapes and pixels. I watch clean animated lines from the late 1980s and early 1990s. I could make a whole false world here, a comforting one, with bustle and excitement but also bounded, safe, and never *in extremis* even as it courts extremity. That is Rilke now, the extremity I know ends somewhere.

I think this is katabasis, still, the descent. I think I have to keep going down. I don't have a golden bough, but a white-painted palm frond from the little sculpture show at the Gagosian just before the virus hit, the one wherein I looked at Twombly *things*, little white graves and memories, and was then, less than moved. But now? Now I wave a makeshift stick ship, with the names of the three Boeotian muses in his spidery hand, I wave it like a talisman, strung up with catkins. When I get to the realm of the Shades, if I am granted admission, I will look for Thyrsis of Etna, the one with the tuneful voice. I will put my lips to his, give him the usurped kiss of the mouth I have stolen from the upper world, and then let him sing. I will turn back continually, and we will not attempt to leave at all, not yet anyway.

The first of the *Sonnets To Orpheus*, the end of the third and the fourth lines:

> ... Doch selbst in der Verschweigung
> Ging neuer Anfang, Wink, und Wandlung vor.

> ... Yet even in this silence
> Came new starting, signs, and metamorphoses.

Nothing here is new actually, it is all old as Hadrian, as the white-blank eyes of the Gods, as the oars of the little ships. If I must change my life it is only the old change, the grooves worn into the fields and footnotes. Yet, it is silent. Yet, yet the old becomes less trite or angry or teenaged when it is allowed to unfurl here, Wandlung wandering.

Maybe neon still makes Prometheus groan with recognition as he awaits every day the eagle. Rilke, I think, admires the avidity with which the pointed beak of the bird attacks the liver.

2.

Sometimes the study is better than the finished thing as it is here, suffused with longing. The provisionality of the study leaves room for it to be free. Right now, like time and the future, language is also provisional, so provisional and free that it feels like you might fall off of something huge and intractable every time you write a sentence.

There is danger here, with passion, the same frisson as always but configured anew. No one is touching anyone's strange body.

Rilke does something for me now. Does my writing about Rilke do anything for anybody? Does it have to? Is second-order art by nature secondary and therefore unnecessary, un-essential. We use the word essential a lot lately; workers, equipment, ventilators, masks. Essential for upkeep of the body, for not being dead. Does criticism keep anyone from dying but critics, we the parasites, feeding on the art to make reviews and essays in the papers? So what if it doesn't. It keeps us alive, the tapeworms, maggots, fig wasps. We fight to thrive too. In a world without maggots, corpses never turn to dust, to ashes, to grass. Without wasps there are no more figs. The Necropolis would starve. But this model of fig-making too, is provisional, hopeful, for who does not want to be necessary in times of necessity?

To be a luxury is a kind of sin, to be disposable. We all want to be well-disposed. We want to live in a world that desires figs and permits us fig wasps in the process. The Lapith and Centaur metope saw the plague of Athens first-hand, saw the death of Pericles, and remained necessary, essential. The Lapiths and Centaurs were all dust by its first construction anyway, and by the Plague, in the fifth century BCE? Memories. And now, memory of a memory, in the now-quiet galleries of the British Museum, dust gathers on the Lapiths' helmets and Centaurs' spear-tips, and in the open mouths of braying horses, fixed in marble, living dead. Perhaps they will give lessons, the metopes, in how to live frozen over, in the thick morass of time. I could use one, such a lesson.

Day and night and days and weeks blur. I wonder, if like the women in Ovid, I have become a tree to escape something, someone. But I look down at my hands in the park and they aren't branches yet, just warm and thudding flesh in the new catacombs of streets, sirens, flats. Seeds in a cut pomegranate.

3.

I move the hands in the arms of my giant robot body, trying futilely to turn the mecha of myself; the bodies from which we are now alienated and yet encased. Archaic torsos without arms anymore. I am going down. I take small steps like melting 19th century cityscape. Debussy, Chopin, Satie. Metropole made of ice-cream, sliding. The city or the Necropolis, neither feels real. Katabasis is backwards in spring. It is supposed to be winter. Maybe if we write in the backwards part of the boustrephedon everything will make sense again. The government keeps calling it 'the new normal'. I keep sliding, keep reading Rilke.

'Orpheus. Eurydike. Hermes'
Rilke, translated from the German by Stephen Mitchell
Neue Gedichte (1907)

Das war der Seelen wunderliches
    Bergwerk.
Wie stille Silbererze gingen sie
als Adern durch sein Dunkel.
    Zwischen Wurzeln
entsprang das Blut, das fortgeht zu
    den Menschen,
und schwer wie Porphyr sah es aus
    im Dunkel.
Sonst war nichts Rotes.

That was the deep uncanny mine of
    souls.
Like veins of silver ore, they silently
moved through its massive darkness.
    Blood welled up
among the roots, on its way to the world
    of men,
and in the dark it looked as hard as
    stone.
Nothing else was red.

Rilke says *Porphyry*, here, and not just stone. All the porphyry in the world came from one quarry in Egypt, Pliny tell us. They lost the quarry around the 5th century BCE. They did not find it again until the 19th century, 1820, which was before Rilke, but meant that all the porphyry in renaissance and medieval churches is *spolia*, spoils from somewhere else, sometimes refashioned sarcophagi. Porphyry looks a little like dried blood, but it's what the Byzantines meant when they say someone was born in the purple. Chopping up sarcophagi to make altars for the new gods, how very delightful, easy, even. It is too easy to make something of this here. The *deep mine of souls* is perhaps not in this manner analogized; the Bergwerk, the mountain-work, ore-works pulling stone and little metal veins out of the earth, spoliating it in open pits that were churches to the sky. That is, a memorial to falling, to heights, to aftermaths.

I look at a print, but a print that looks like a study or a sketch, called 'Orphee entrainant Eurydice', Orpheus leading Eurydice, by Corot, 1860. It is after porphyry and before Rilke. He grabs a lyre from the tree. Groups of other souls cluster, huddle almost on the paths. The forest of the underworld is all sticks and crosshatching, thick nets of black on the off-white paper. A sketch leaves room, the possibility of the provisional, but it also *casts out*, forbids. The light does not enter here, in this place which is paradoxically all somehow a shadow, burin on wavering pen. It could be a Parisian garden, this, but there is a wildness there, an unforgivingness in the realm of the Shades. Cue the soundtrack: Satie. Debussy. Chopin; the nocturnes.

The dead, too, have a city.

Rilke feels petulant sometimes because he is so dramatic that there is no ordinary. But this is no ordinary anymore, so he is admitted, as I crawl down the world for spring. I like aftermaths.

4.

There is a moment when the sea draws back, breathes and drains out before a crashing wave comes in to pull you under, when you can see everything there, even the bottom. Once, when I was a child, at low tide on a tiny island off Florida in the Gulf of Mexico, the water was thick with swimming rays. My father offered to carry me past them into the sea, where the currents pull you down and out and you have to remember to swim sideways, because it will pull you down, the sea; it is infallible that way.

Halfway out I asked to be put in the midst of the school of rays. The sun beat on my back, the sunscreen washing away slowly into the creases of my knees and elbows. The rays swam around my legs, glancing them softly, doing nothing. They felt exactly and strangely like velvet, brushing up against my bare skin.

Felsen waren da
und wesenlose Wälder. Brücken über
    Leeres
und jener große graue blinde Teich,
der über seinem fernen Grunde hing
wie Regenhimmel über einer
    Landschaft.
Und zwischen Wiesen, sanft und
    voller Langmut,
erschien des einen Weges blasser
    Streifen,
wie eine lange Bleiche hingelegt.

There were cliffs there,
and forests made of mist. There were
    bridges
spanning the void, and that great gray
    blind lake
which hung above its distant bottom
like the sky on a rainy day above a
    landscape.
And through the gentle, unresisting
    meadows
one pale path unrolled like a strip of
cotton.

I think of the path there as made of rays too, and it is not a lake but a small, salted sea. And when you get out of the mists, when you are Eurydike and you are dead, the rays let you walk on their backs, because you are inside the ripcurrent, already under. The pale path of their backs glows gently in the inverse light and you carry a lantern like a delighted child, Eurydike. When Orpheus comes to get you he knows nothing of this. He sees the sadness of your winding cloths, fresh from the tomb. You see white dresses and pale pink flowers in the evening, just in the gloaming of dusk, and the paper globes of the lanterns flickering that make you born anew here, here where everyone is a child. To you, though, on the gentle meadow that feels like a rolling cut brocade in silk, it is cast in the soft purpling of the underhilled sun. This is not the red-purple of porphyry, but a Singer Sargent lilac evening, the evening of a dream — *Carnation, Lily, Lily, Rose*.

Sometimes I think Twombly's flowers, the ones where he uses Rilke, are a little blousy, a little bit the memory of Singer Sargent's when you're forty and have two small children of your own, running in the meadows. But my pale path isn't there yet; I am somewhere between the rays and now. Dead air, blind lake, the not-knowing-what-is-coming extends before me and I can only walk with everyone else's memories.

5.

Orpheus does not see it this way at all. In the land of the living, there is no in between, only the veil to the dead, and after. If he comes back up again, back with you, it is because the veil tears. Twombly's *Treatise On The Veil* is the same. It is based on a piece of music concrète from 1953, *Le Voile d'Orphée*, by Pierre Henry. You can hear cotton tearing when Orpheus goes down into the underworld as you listen to the track. In turn, Twombly made the final piece, dark and durational but with hints of the chalkboard paintings, *in continuo*. I don't like *Treatise On The Veil*, not really, but I love many of the sketches for it, the rectangles marked for time and pressed hard by crayons and pastels, varying shades of filled up, grey and black but also even green or a lapis blue. Some of them even glow a ghostly white, or a cast-lit white, like the back of the rays, or like the cotton path. They're paint chips for an infinite and unfinished room.

Do we have to hate the undertow if it is beautiful, even if it draws us down into the quiet world of the dead? Maybe it's not the dead, but a hallway space, and the winding cloths, the winding cloths aren't fearful but succoring, like quilts on a crisp fall night, like a vast silk cocoon.

Metamorphosing is terrifying— for wasps inside dark outlets of figs, for tapeworms, for moths; for Persephone it is rape. If you wind yourself up in cotton are you protected? Is there a talisman somehow?

In the British Museum there is indeed a talisman; a gold case necklace, with a leaf of gold inside incised with letters. It is called the Petelia Gold Tablet, from late Rome but before Constantine and the incidents at the Milvian Bridge. The inscription, in the style of Greek epigraphy on stone, runs together like this, all the letters knitted into a single path or back:

1. ΕΥΡΗΣΣΕΙΣΔΑΙΔΑΟΔΟΜΩΝΕΠΑΡΙΣΤΕΡΑΚΡΗΝ

2. ΗΝΠΑΡΔΑΥΤΗΙΛΕΥΚΗΝΕΣΤΗΚΥΙΑΝΚΥΠΑΡΙΣΣΟΝ

3. ΤΑΥΤΗΣΤΗΣΚΡΗΝΗΣΜΗΔΕΣΧΕΔΟΝΕΜΠΕΛΑΣΕΙΑΣ

4. ΕΥΡΕΗΣΕΙΣΔΕΤΕΡΑΝΤΗΣΜΝΗΜΟΣΥΝΗΣΑΠΟΛΙΜΝΗΣ

5. ΨΥΧΡΟΝΥΔΩΡΠΡΟΡΕΟΝΦΥΛΑΚΕΣΔΕΠΙΠΡΟΣΘΕΝΕΑΣΙΝ

6. ΕΙΠΕΙΝΓΗΣΠΑΙΣΕΙΜΙΚΑΙΟΥΡΑΝΟΥΑΣΤΕΡΟΕΝΤΟΣΑΥΤΑΡΕΜ

7. ΟΙΓΕΝΟΣΟΥΡΑΝΙΟΝΤΟΔΕΔΙΣΤΕΚΑΙΑΥΤΟΙΔΙΨΗΙΔΕΙΜΙΑΥ

8. ΗΚΑΙΑΠΟΛΛΥΜΑΙΑΛΛΑΔΟΤΑΙΨΑΨΥΧΡΟΝΥΔΩΡΠΡΟΡΕ

9. ΟΝΤΗΣΜΝΗΜΟΣΥΝΗΣΑΠΟΛΙΜΝΗΣΚΑΥΤ[. .]Σ[.]
ΙΔΩΣΟΥΣΙ
10. ΠΙΕΙΝΘΕΙΗΣΑΠ[. .]ΝΗΣΚΑΙΤΟΤΕΠΕΙΤΑ[………]
ΗΡΩΕ
11. ΣΣΙΝΑΝΑΞΕΙ[[…………]ΝΗΣΤΟΔΕΙ [
12. ΘΑΝΕΙΣΘ[………………….]ΟΔΕΓΡΑ[
• in right margin: ΤΟΓΛΩΣΕΙΠΑΣΚΟΤΟΣΑΜΦΙΚΑΛΥΨΑΣ

1. You will find in the halls of Hades a spring on the left,
2. and standing by it, a glowing white cypress tree;
3. Do not approach this spring at all.
4. You will find another, from the lake of Memory
5. refreshing water flowing forth. But guardians are nearby.
6. Say: "I am the child of Earth and starry Heaven;
7. But my race is heavenly; and this you know yourselves.
8. I am parched with thirst and I perish; but give me quickly
9. refreshing water flowing forth from the lake of Memory."
10. And then they will give you to drink from the divine spring,
11. And then you will celebrate? [rites? with the other] heroes.
12. This [is the ? … of Memory, when you are about] to die . .
• in right margin: ……].?? shadow covering around[1]

This, this is a stick painted Twombly white and full of golden catkins. This tells us how to pass. But what if we don't want to? What if we stay by the glowing white cypress, and drink from that spring instead? This is an Orphic rite. What does a Eurydic one look like, if like her we keep going down and do

---

1   Transcription from Smith, Cecil, and D. Comparetti. " The Petelia Gold Tablet." The Journal of Hellenic Studies, vol. 3, 1882, pp. 111 — 118.

not turn back? What if we are not ready to remember how to be whole and alive yet? I want to stay in katabasis for a while, soak up the underiver of the world.

One of the studies for *Treatise On The Veil* was done in 1970. It is almost all white, with thin black lines indicating notes and footsteps. In the description of its materials, the catalogue notes that it is held together only by Scotch tape. If the veil is held together by a thin strip of cellophane does it really sound like cotton when you tear it? Is it really that chorus of dense innumerable blacks the painting is, and not the sketch? Provisionally, this veil is more permeable, membranous. Provisionally you can slip inside it like a screen left open a crack, or a shoji screen that slides on oiled bamboo.

I am a child of Earth and Starry Heaven.

Maybe, but I am also a child of the glowing white tree, of the tide pulled back. ΚΥΠΑΡΙΣΣΟΝ— cypress. Cypress oil smells clean and almost medicinal when it's laid on wood to protect wool and sweaters from moths. They take you into the winter, sweaters, layered on cashmere like a chrysalis. They take you into spring, the memory-smell of the tree, the table scrap, the sculpture; a blousy flower.

Und dieses einen Weges kamen sie. Down this path they were coming.

What is written in the golden tablet case that hangs around your neck? In another 1970 study for *Treatise*, Twombly plans the (eventually 33-foot-long) painting on a small piece of paper. There are four rectangles, each variously shaded with a bright, almost oceanic blue. The second one, marked at something like 30.4 with a 2 above and some other crossed out notation, has a quick dash of semi-translucent lilac on it, as if to show the rays of sun peeking through, or a light, maybe, a lantern. It is about the size of a business card, and you could carry it easily there, where your aortic pulse thrums closest to the skin. You could trace the small purple line, the dashed off glance of light, through the rolled paper and the weight of the chain. It is just becoming evening, or maybe dawn; you could say it like a prayer or consternation or even contradictory defiance, under the thicket of dark branches in the print of the underworld's woods by Corot. Orpheus may not see it there, but she does and you do, and maybe even Twombly did in that sketch, or just left room for us to. The cypress tree; the other turn; the changing Eurydike (*Carnation, Lily, Lily, Rose?*). When the light is between designated hours this is the hour of our metamorphosing, the unformed and currently forming, those both dead and still living off fumes and poems— we're all moths here full of last season's wool; we're all possibility, provisionals, studies for the anabasis to come that makes us whole again, or at least maybe seeming so.

6.

Voran der schlanke Mann im blauen
Mantel,
der stumm und ungeduldig vor sich
aussah.
Ohne zu kauen fraß sein Schritt den
Weg
in großen Bissen; seine Hände hingen
schwer und verschlossen aus dem
Fall der Falten
und wußten nicht mehr von der
leichten Leier,
die in die Linke eingewachsen war
wie Rosenranken in den Ast des
Ölbaums.
Und seine Sinne waren wie entzweit:
indes der Blick ihm wie ein Hund
vorauslief,
umkehrte, kam und immer wieder
weit

Infront, the slender man in the blue cloak
— mute, impatient, looking straight
ahead.
In large, greedy, unchewed bites his
walk
devoured the path; his hands hung at
his sides,
tight and heavy, out of the falling
folds,
no longer conscious of the delicate
lyre
which had grown into his left arm,
like a slip
of roses grafted onto an olive tree.
His senses felt as though they were
split in two;
his sight would race ahead of him like

und wartend an der nächsten
   Wendung stand,—
blieb sein Gehör wie ein Geruch
   zurück.
Manchmal erschien es ihm als
   reichte es
bis an das Gehen jener beiden andern,
die folgen sollten diesen ganzen
   Aufstieg.
Dann wieder wars nur seines Steigens
   Nachklang
und seines Mantels Wind was hinter
   ihm war.

a dog,
stop, come back, then rushing off
   again
would stand, impatient, at the path's
   next turn,—
but his hearing, like an odor, stayed
   behind.
Sometimes it seemed to him as
   though it reached
back to the footsteps of those other two
who were to follow him, up the long
   path home.
But then, once more, it was just his own
   steps' echo,
or the wind inside his cloak, that made
   the sound.

I am neither slender, nor a man, but I both read and walk in eager, gulping steps now. Spring turns into summer, racing ahead. One day, on an aimless path across Regents' Park, I end up in Queen Mary's Rose Garden. I did not go there much before, since when the roses were in bloom and it was summer, which invariably meant the sun beat down and it smelled of tourists and shit. Roses are picky that way, they need to be fertilized. But this is an odd rainy start of summer, and there are no tourists here now, now that we are in the Necropolis or the halfway place to it that the world has paused to become. The Necropolis loves its roses.

I wonder idly how hard it would be to graft an olive to a rose. Before, I would have told you I just wanted the olive, a crown of her leaves, to say, and say more, the way mythic poets did with lyres. This was a childish dream and grafts are a tricky business. I once wrote about how in the gardens of the seventeenth century Palatinate, the same gardens that were shelled to nothingness even in their nascent completion, the oranges were not grafted. This was a miracle akin to the singing automata in sacred caverns, these un-grafted oranges, pampered still by a glasshouse, but rooted then in German soil. "Wurzeln"—roots—" Bergwerk"— mountain-work, mining— Rilke knows this problem too, I think, a place that grows roses more easily than oranges, where the wind whips sometimes and it is cold enough for a woolen cloak.

I find myself admiring the roses now, loose with their petals, soft on the keys adjacent like the Debussy or Chopin. Twombly's roses feel grafted too, those late in life paintings, the ones that like the flowers, people seem to irrationally love. I like them better now that I see them through seeing *Treatise On A Veil*. They seem to be in sequence, not a bed of roses, but one rose blossoming, wilting, dying along the split axis of time. Here Twombly uses the French Rilke, because people think French is more romantic than German, supposedly— another thing I have failed to understand. In the 2008 series, there are always three roses on the oversized horizontal plane of the canvas. In *The Rose (I)* all three are yellow-orange, in *II* they are more yellow but overlined in a way that is fearsome, dripping red like blood. *III* are a purple-black, the petals overlaid in the same flash yellow as Lepanto, *IV* a more traditional fulsome red but with flaming centers. All three roses in *V* drip black.

This, in turn, reminds me of the roses of Heliogabalus, one of those mad emperors, the ones that Twombly thought about during the Commodus paintings, I'm sure. Alma-Tadema thought of Heliogabalus   in 1888 (just before the newly rediscovered porphyry, all that red, came out of the mines again). Supposedly, Heliogabalus had a dinner party where guests were showered in roses and violets, and there were so many roses that some drowned to death in them, suffocated by spent blossoms. This was probably based on a story about Nero from Suetonius, but who cares anyway, the way that Alma-Tadema paints them, wild, ecstatic even in their death. The petals riot. There are glimpses of faces, struggling to gasp for breath. You can tell though, that like Twombly in his later years at Gaeta, Alma-Tadema thought it was maybe a beautiful thing to die this way, to bloom so fully and completely that one is subsumed into the rose.

But wait, my senses run ahead of me like a dog now, split. I am holding something back from you. This is what I can do with roses, give you the runaround, which is also true, also criticism but similarly a decorative fiction. There is something else. Shhh! We have not yet turned back! Do not take my breath from me with a petal— yet!

7.

I am going to skip some verses now, to pin where the poem turns. I, too, am turning:

Den Gott des Ganges und der weiten
    Botschaft,
die Reisehaube über hellen Augen,
den schlanken Stab hertragend vor
    dem Leibe
und flügelschlagend an den
    Fußgelenken;
und seiner linken Hand gegeben: *sie*.

[...]

Sie aber ging an jenes Gottes Hand,
den Schrittbeschränkt von langen
    Leichenbändern,

The god of speed and distant messages,
a traveler's hood above his shining eyes,
his slender staff held out in front of him,
and little wings fluttering at his ankles;
and on his left arm, barely touching it:
she...
[...]
But now she walked beside the graceful
    god,
her steps constricted by the trailing
graveclothes,
uncertain, gentle, and without
    impatience.

unsicher, sanft und ohne Ungeduld.
Sie war in sich, wie Eine hoher
    Hoffnung,
und dachte nicht des Mannes, der
    voranging,
und nicht des Weges, der ins Leben
    aufstieg.
Sie war in sich. Und ihr Gestorbensein
    erfüllte sie wie Fülle.
Wie eine Frucht von Süßigkeit und
    Dunkel,
so war sie voll von ihrem großen Tode,
der also neu war, daß sie nichts begriff.

[...]

Sie war schon aufgelöst wie langes
    Haar
und hingegeben wie gefallner Regen
und ausgeteilt wie hundertfacher
    Vorrat.

Sie war schon Wurzel.

Und als plötzlich jäh
der Gott sie anhielt und mit Schmerz
    im Ausruf
die Worte sprach: Er hat sich
    umgewendet—,
begriff sie nichts und sagte leise:
    Wer?

Fern aber, dunkel vor dem klaren
    Ausgang,
stand irgend jemand, dessen Angesicht
nicht zu erkennen war. Er stand und
    sah,
wie auf dem Streifen eines
    Wiesenpfades

She was deep within herself, like a
    woman heavy
with child, and did not see the man in
    front
or the path ascending steeply into life.
Deep within herself. Being dead
filled her beyond fulfillment. Like a
fruit suffused with its own mystery and
    sweetness,
she was filled with her vast death, which
    was so new,
she could not understand that it had
    happened.

[...]

She was already loosened like
    long hair,
poured out like fallen rain,
shared like a limitless supply.

She was already root.

And when, abruptly,
the god put out his hand to stop her,
    saying,
with sorrow in his voice: He has
    turned around—,
she could not understand, and softly
answered: *Who?*

    Far away,
dark before the shining exit-gates,
someone or other stood, whose
    features were

mit trauervollem Blick der Gott der
    Botschaft
sich schweigend wandte, der Gestalt zu
    folgen,
die schon zurückging dieses selben
    Weges,
den Schritt beschränkt von langen
    Leichenbändern,
unsicher, sanft und ohne Ungeduld.

unrecognizable. He stood and saw
how, on the strip of road among the
    meadows,
with a mournful look, the god of
    messages
silently turned to follow the small figure
already walking back along the path,
her steps constricted by the trailing
    graveclothes,
uncertain, gentle, and without
    impatience.

Oh he thinks she is uncertain, fragile like a rose! But the rose is the provisional thing, the sketch, for the bromeliad, whose leaves cup in a hot tropical forest a whole engendered world, frogs and eggs and gnats rising up from the trapped rain. The Bromeliad Eurydice is not gentle for all her seeming impatience. She does not say "Who?" out of indifference but because of what she has become, a spiky inflorescence climbing out of wet primeval leaves in the peated ground, dark under the canopy. Rilke mourns for Orpheus. Orpheus gets torn apart by maenads or animals for being a pederast. Orpheus is not long for the living anyway. Orpheus cannot return whole. Forget being Orpheus.

"Who?"

But Eurydice? What has she found in the new vastness of her death? Sweetness is only meek when you can't drown in flowers, in a world without Heliogabalus or banquets or Twombly or time, slipping and marching. The wells in bromeliads, incidentally breed mosquitoes, the females of which are the ones who suck up blood, exemplary parasites.

Let's call this the Eurydic rite, the one where we refuse to come back up. We make a home here on the flat path of the underworldly plain, our Necropolis, our school of velveteen rays. We live as much in death than in living now. And when a god comes to us in a traveler's hood and winks we know exactly when to play it dumb. Tear all the cloth. Dance in your winding clothes. Put down roots, grow with the hungry hybridity of the graft. Feed with your needle mouth on the rich porphyry veins of the world. To write or read on the precipice feels right in this moment in particular, as if it is coming into a new fullness, a wholeness which was not possibly entirely in the complacency of our living before, the city whose obverse was not at Necropolis yet. This is the moment when the skin of the fig gives into the needle of the wasp's thorax, when the wasp breaks into the dark.

Alone in the beds of flowers, in the long summer evening in Regent's Park, I write out two new initials in petals, an unexpected thing. There is a girl on the other side of the night now, tentative, for this is the tentativeness we see in walking here, a tentativeness of allowing ourselves to feel again. Is this for us, or only for the living? Who are the living, and who truly, the dead? When I write about Rilke I re-animate him, drag up his shade for a chat. Or maybe I send myself down, down there, and decide to stay or at least get a passport. The Necropolis is my city too now, one in which the white roots of the daytime world are all coming up roses, that crush or bloom invariably their own craterous timelines, in which the tentative is everything, the animate risk of the cell.

The catkins have split open and dropped their pollen into the air and on the ground, and they are growing back small and green again. I send Chiron an email on winged feet.

I think I am falling in love again.

There is no centaur's medicine for that.

PART 4

1.

"J'ai fait juste un bisou" !!!

"I just kissed [it]!" "It was only a kiss"

One of Twombly's early classical paintings, from the year 1959, is called *The Age Of Alexander*. The painting is named superficially for Alexander of Macedon, of whom pretty much everyone knows the paraphrase of the Plutarch quote that he wept when he had no more worlds left to conquer, and usually not much else. Cy Twombly's infant son, born the same year the painting was made, is named Cyrus Alessandro. The Alessandro is for this same Alexander, the one who laid claim to the Persians and beyond. The Cyrus is for the Persian king Alexander himself admired, who conquered the Lydians and the Medes, but then unified them under a (supposedly) pluralistic rule. Alexander knew about Cyrus from Xenophon, whose *Anabasis* he avidly read. The Anabasis is about a bunch of Greek shock troops clawing their way back to the sea. It is the technical opposite of *katabasis*, which is a descent, like Orpheus going down.

I have three things in common with the Alexander for whom I was most decidedly not named: I am short, I am stubborn, and my first love was Homer. I slept with a copy of the *Iliad* under my pillow at the same surly adolescent age he was made a cavalry commander. I did this until the same age as when Alexander was a general under his father Philip, who conquered Attica, and in some ways tried to be more Greek than the Greeks. This too, I have tried, with middling success. Not the part about conquering Attica, but the part of wanting to be more Greek than the Greeks, of wanting some mythical dead Athens to love me as I loved that copy of Robert Fagles's translation, bound in stripes of metallic blue, reminiscent of a vase, with false French cut pages that were the height of mass-market paperback luxury. I wanted to have the *Iliad* love me, as a wasp wants love from a fig, which is to say it is both impossible and somehow true. The wasp dies and is born inside the fig, and the I that writes this was born inside that translation of Homer and will die there someday too.

We always go back to Homer, or I do, the I who wants to be the authoritative we. I have also always been late to Homer, that same belatedness that creeps up everywhere again. In this country, young British boys of means learn Greek and Latin from holders of prestigious Oxbridge doctorates, in the medieval halls of the Public Schools, starting at ten or eleven. I have made no secret of always envying this, but surely, like much else, I would have hated it. Anyway, at fourteen to seventeen, I was already too late. Alexander was late to Homer too, born

356 BCE in Pella, which is very rocky and far and not Athens. Our aims were admittedly different—Alexander wanted to be Achilles. I just wanted to sit under my duvet and read.

I may or may not have kissed that *Iliad*, but I didn't wear lipstick then. The last thing I kissed with lipstick on was the envelope edges of a letter I sent last week to the girl across the sea, the one whose initials I spelled in petals in the rose garden. It was admittedly trite. Perhaps that is what made Rindy Sam's act in the gallery memorable though, that it was a trite thing, that same kind of red-pink kiss planted on the Twombly white. It was so obviously sacrilege, so obviously devotion, so obviously desire. In this obviousness it remains for me a living wound.

The difference between Alexander's troops and Greek hoplites of a previous generation partly lay in speed and horses, and partly in weapons. The Macedonian *sarissa* differs in the following ways from the Hoplite spear: it was held horizontally toward the front, but reached further because it was longer, it was used with pikes to hold the back of a formation, and it was held by the infantry front line in overlapping, simultaneous layers that bristle out like spikes.

On the leftmost side of *The Age Of Alexander*, which reads like a campaign across Persia from left to right, there are three twisted rectangles, from longest to shortest, labeled 2, 3, and 4. There is also a 1 that seems to have been partially effaced. Perhaps, as has been argued elsewhere, those were references to Twombly's mathematical work as an army cryptographer, that some see in the sine-like waves later on, on the right. Perhaps they are units or single bodies twisting in the wind. Below them are three triangles, jutting out like the prows of his later simplified drawings of ships. They could be just coming to some rocky beach, having crossed the choppy Aegean Sea. The prows and the rectangles are both neat lead pencil, not yet as scrawled as the central picture plane, almost delicate still. What if they were sarissas, held up to the sky, twisting in the wind?

I don't know what Twombly did and didn't know about sarissas, or about love, in 1959. Here it does not matter to me, or matters slantwise just now. Some later day I will tell you about his marriage, his lover, his son, about Hephaestion and Alexander and the Persian boy, and all the facts I could marshal here, in tight blocky lines, spears pitched. Someday but not today, not here—we have wounds to do.

Did you know that some mosquitoes numb you before they bite, so you don't slap them? Did you know that tapeworms secrete immunosuppressant chemicals so your body doesn't force them out? Did you know when you stab a man with a sarissa you hope it cuts him clean through, that it doesn't get stuck, that after the battle men lay on the flat trampled ground there, groaning, begging for death or crying out for aid? That in the same part of the painting there is a first, light red scrawl like a wound, like a dime-store lipstick kiss red? Did you know when you finally pull the head of the sarissa, the ridged tip, out of a man's shoulder or groin, where the gaps in his armour were, that he often bleeds out and dies from this very wish to live?

If he does live, the man pierced by the sarissa, and if the wound heals and he does not die of splinters or sepsis or sheer shock, it doesn't often heal clean. It heals as a great mound of raised tissue, a lead or wax pencil scrawl against the paint-smooth surface of the skin. There are so many of these on the surface of *The Age Of Alexander*, these battles sites or wounds scarred over, that they seem countless. Alexander was wounded like this himself several times, and the later historical accounts, dubious though they are, make some point or another about his superhuman ability to withstand pain and heal.

Someday if I am dead on a pyre you can count the wounds on my back, between the ribs of the upper left, past the knitted tissue that holds them there and into the heart. I have small round scars on my décolletage—such a delicate word for a battlefield, that!—where I used to pick my skin clean until it bled. Those are dead tumuli now.

But on my back, none of those die. These wounds are neither literal nor superficial. They are the part of me that does not know Alexander, that has no name like Alexander, that only remembers the blank searing pain of the man pulling the tip of the sarissa out and the fast rush of blood, lipstick on white oil made to look simple like housepaint, because simplicity makes it easier, somehow, the starkness of it.

Today, the Girl from Across the Sea pulled out the sarissa, and I wept. I did not want to conquer any worlds. There are scars there now, two cities raised in seismographic lines, like the ones on *The Age Of Alexander*'s right, the peaks sometimes labeled too in a cryptic and partial numerical script. One scar is covered over, almost illegible. The other bleeds and bleeds onto the clean rolling linens, leftwise to right.

Sometimes a thing men do on the field of battle—for we read it in Arrian and in Xenophon, when we read about Alexander—sometimes a thing men do—is to ask for water even though they know they are wounded and going to die, immobile and extending their death. Sometimes their enemies, thinking it a kindness, a dignity, finish them quickly instead.

"*J'ai fait juste un bisou*" !!!

The red-pink lipstick kiss, the edges of the upper and lower lip, the wound on the canvas made in the act of love, in desperation; this has no dignity. It begs for water, knowing it will die. It lets itself be carried in a litter off the field, to groan in some dark tent. You could gauge its severity, label it, figure it, 2, 3, 4. But in the end it wouldn't matter, to me at least.

If it were you, I would look into your eyes while you brought a blade between the fixed and unfixed vertebrae of my neck, a rectangle, a white square of cartilage giving and twisting.

If it were her, if she reads this now still, I simply say: pour. I am undignified. I want the segmented worm of my love to struggle on, to live, if only a few minutes more. For her alone, this, flailing.

There are more things desperate than just love. No one said anabasis would be easy, fighting your way like Cyrus back to the sea. So much depends, for the young Alexander, on his scrolls of Homer kept in a sturdy leathern case. So much depends on a kiss. So much depends now on these dependent acts, parasitic and devoid of a certain dignity, that are critical acts too. I draw my finger against the photograph of the painting in a glossy catalogue, that field of scratches and scars, peaks and dents, all that time drawn out. I open the Arrian, the Xenophon. I read like there is nothing left to conquer, just as I have wept, as there is red-fresh blood, that makes me new again, trickling down my back; a history painting.

2.

Don't kill your darlings, march them across Persia.

Trust me it will be worse than dying. By the end they'll hate you for having done it, having taken them to Issus first, which in *The Age of Alexander* looks something like a closed door with a diagonal slash of scribbled lead-gray rending it open. By the time of Alexander, by my time keeping, by a certain lateness to Homer, a lateness from which one can never recover, really, your darlings start to feel uncomfortable anyway, like you're a fish with a louse for a tongue that has realized only just now it's not a tongue for a tongue.

Am I "over interpreting" this painting? Probably. It certainly meant nothing about wounds and fish louses to Cy Twombly. Were I writing an historical or academic argument I would have to care then, about the boundary conditions for believability, for perceived intent, and for context. Whatever this is, I've now called them off. I can say anything, which is nothing so much as dangerously overwhelming. I do this all the time to the whole world; see it as a layering of partially readable signs and portents, like some unlucky augur forever staring into the guts of sheep, the flightpath of certain birds. This often calls for melodrama, especially when the drama of the world as it really is doesn't result in any kind of expected catharsis, Aristotelian or otherwise. I map myself onto whatever interpretation I've divined for that day, that hour, and then map myself back onto the world again in another looping cycle.

I see *The Age of Alexander* when I close my eyes at night now, and when I am out in the small hours, supposedly running. The other night I was going down a side street near the hill when I almost bodied into Cappuccino. Cappuccino is one of the two foxes, the other is Flat White. I named them for coffee types in the deepest of lockdown winter, when I so desperately wanted a coffee shop that I manifested it onto the texture of their fur (frothy) or its shade (Flat White, predictably, has a white tip at the end of her tail). I think Cappuccino is male because I didn't see him with kits, but anyway, I dismiss the idea that he is a *kitsune*, the Japanese fox sprite of a transformed lover. You don't name an implacable spirit Cappuccino by accident, you just don't, and anyway we both jump into the air and yelp at our unexpected meeting. They don't scare from me as easily, now, the foxes, but we were both surprised.

The problem with seeing signs and portents everywhere, with reading the world like a book, is that it starts to echo and drive you crazy slowly. Anyway, I don't kill my darlings, in writing or otherwise. That advice came from *Faulkner* of all people, who would be smug about it, the bastard. If I killed my darlings there would be nothing left, they're all darlings, all of them, the stories I tell myself about the world. They're the infrastructure too, a kind of scaffolding, in which the other things are cradled. So Cappuccino is not a *kitsune* but that doesn't mean he's not a symbol, the potentate of his own little foxy empire of meaning between the bins.

For about three consecutive days I watch an unbelievably camp Spanish heist show on Netflix. There are no black and white tiles. My bangs drip down into my eyes now, and I need to cut them, so I cut them like the fast and loose protagonist, inexplicably yet explicably named for a major Japanese city. I apply a new shade of lipstick from the armory, this one a slow-burn kind of brown rose, a rose with some sort of fungal infection. I like that, the potential for corruption. It's in *The Age Of Alexander*, too, like so many paintings conceived that same hot summer in Rome, in Twombly's somewhat obvious scrawl toward the lower middle of the canvas: "Death". Well, isn't that helpful. No over interpretation there, I think.

Everything moves slowly, like time does when you're swimming underwater, holding your breath at the bottom of the pool. I send out some emails to friends, mentors, editors. It's hot and gummy. I think of how long oils take to actually dry down, how even in the summer of 1959 in scorching high temperatures, it would have been a while. There are layers and layers of white over wax crayon and pencil and then penciled over again here. The painting, too, feels slow. The Spanish robbers inch about in their red jumpsuits, going nowhere. I myself forgo all extremity. I am trying to figure out how to shift from loved to not loved faster than a blink, an email, a call, a letter. I am reckoning with the possible disparities in the accounts of Arrian. I wonder idly: Why do we name swords but not wounds?

If you look closely, above 'DEath' in *The Age of Alexander* is the word "floods" in small caps, underlined darkly. Next to it is a particularly vivid, scratchy patch of black. The painting is iterative; it suggests the passage of time as it moves across the canvas. I am just trying to remember what time is, besides ticks along an x-axis, first and second derivatives with respect to speed or velocity or armies in motion, whole wings wheeling to envelop each other dangerously, from the vulnerable back and sides. It is Cyrus, a Persian king, who hires the Greeks in Xenophon's account, and it is another Persian king that betrays them. Xenophon blames the satrap of Lydia, Tissaphernes for supporting Artaxerxes, then briefly defecting. He in turn betrays the Greeks who will not surrender to him, by beheading some at a feast, which he uses as barter to get back in the good graces of Artaxerxes again. Xenophon finds this perfidy very un-Greek of him; Alexander read Xenophon before himself marching into Persia.

The reader is supposed to hate Tissaphernes the oath breaker, but tell me, who amongst you has never broken an oath, even a small one? I am the Tissaphernes here; I asked the girl across the sea, the one with whom I was briefly and fiercely in love, to break an oath for me. She desired to, and did not. If she had, I would now be considerably happier. Perhaps she would be too. But she is honorable. So I will call this wound Tissaphernes, but not in damning him. His name sounds like a flood for me, with the long s's, the ending like a trawling river. The centaurs weren't Greeks either really, but the Lapiths were—from Thessaly. From left to right, you can see the forms of *The Age of Alexander* shift, from rectangular and vertical, to horizontal lines and triangular peaks, and then finally to contiguous steep curves, something that looks like a candle, a series of disjointed dots. The Macedonians want to go home, to "Greece" which is "civilization" and not Persia. Alexander drags them to the Indus instead, then Persia again, interminable. From left to right, 'civilization' to 'barbarism,' except everything obvious really, except everyone really did smell better. Rose water, dates, pistachios, steep mountain passes, wide disconsolate plains: who could look upon these things and dislike them? Incidentally, that was not the case with Alexander.

I resign myself to the heist show again and give up on working. I tap my fingertips on my own left forearm, Tissapher-nes. Look at the leftmost edge of the canvas center; dot dot dot dot. The Indus valley floods easily. In the water they slog on, waiting still for the after of the after.

3.

The doctor has prescribed me iron supplements; I think of Hesiod. Iron is the last age, after Gold, Silver, Bronze, and the age of heroes aka Troy aka Homer for which I am always too late, even in my haemoglobin. The Greeks that were Hesiod's contemporaries live in the Age of Iron. At the pharmacy counter, through a mask and plexiglass twice confounded, I accidentally ask for lead. The pharmacist fixes me with a long, curious stare.

Lead white is Twombly white. Before his marriage and expensive Italian oils, it was just housepaint, which wasn't allowed to be lead, but children can't accidentally eat oils, in theory at least, so there's probably lead in them to white them out. *The Age of Alexander*, or Cyrus Alessandro Twombly, eventual scion of the Franchetti family and old Roman money, is not an age of housepaint by 1959. You can tell it's oil by a blob that rises off the most visible scar in the painting, to the right of the exact center, almost at eye height. The blob is above a particularly fearsome scratch, or set of scratches. There are three deep scars of black and then one of a red-red, no blue undertones, like the line of red on a seagull's beak. I think this scratch is Gaugamela.

Here's the thing about a library or a museum: it's not a cavalry. You can't order it to do your bidding, deploy it at will. It's not a *pharmakon* either, cure or poison both. I've tried this, the cavalry, the pharmakon; but like all loved things, the books resist. They have their own minds, they don't take orders. And when you are broken in love you just can't cure it by instantly loving something else, which is what you try to do, in front of a painting or a book.

Then the scribbled pencil lines on the battleground or Xerxes or Cyrus or Anna running in front of the train, or whatever choice you make, just hover again over the field of your vision and map themselves onto you instead. The night before the battle at Gaugamela, Arrian tells us, is a near total eclipse of the moon. Aristandros conveniently read the omens as favorable. Maybe he hated it, the moon; that glowing persistent white in a camp full of rustling tent flaps and anxious soldiers, awake at their spits and cauldrons, just waiting, waiting. He mapped the moon onto the situation at hand and said go.

Gaugamela is the decisive battle in the capture of Persia, long before Alexander's troops suffer at Hydaspes, and in India, and feel in victory that they are trapped in defeat. Hephaestion, Alexander's lover, is not yet dead. He rides beside him, golden. Meanwhile the Persians bring a lot of baggage, both literally and figuratively. It is pretty evident Darius does not want to be there, that most of the conscripted troops don't want to be there either, but he doesn't surrender because that is unthinkable. They are silent except when Arrian says they shout, running into battle "Alalai". How different is this from *Bar bar*? The Greeks will never love Alexander in Athens. Anyway, he conquers Persia, or starts to, by commanding at the edge of the right flank. He lets Darius think the left flank is weakening, falling back, but then encircles him from behind, like a chalkboard loop. There is a secret second line in the central phalanx, almost etched into the paint it is so deep, the wax crayon that is supposed to look like the point of a pencil digging in, a deep rhythmic scratch. Alexander takes their chariots.

There is a throwaway line here in Arrian about the Persian troops. He calls a contingent of them the apple-bearers. Think about this the next time you see an apple, red in the produce section, when you bite into the red and see the white flesh underneath, the eclipsed moon of the fruit. "An apple a day keeps the doctor away"—maybe, but the painting isn't your doctor, your therapist, your fifty extended release milligrams of Paxil that you need to function every day, that keep you from going mute. The Apple Bearers were amongst those guarding the royal chariots.

They probably all died. They don't exist even in the little scratches around the big scratch on the field of lead white. They didn't for you. They didn't die for anyone really, for anything, for the absence or presence of something I could love. Don't allow your imagination to think that, to read that in. It will crush you someday, that hope.

Hephaestion is wounded, Alexander's lover. The Companions of Alexander, the cavalry he is able to lean on infallibly here, press in cruelly from the right, wheeling. The wound only makes him angry, like a swarm of bees, like a wasp drilling and drilling into the hard cusp of a fig, he wants now only to live and for Darius to die. Black and white. Wax crayon; oils. More than a thousand horses die on the field. Darius flees. Alexander wins. Some victory, and this is the good one, the one his veterans will brag about when they are mired in swamps (floods) and in the desert later. When Hephaestion dies it will be when Alexander returns to Babylon again, but this time he is triumphant, parading through its streets. Pomegranates, which are apples and moons, sit flush in the hanging gardens. Alexander presses on to Susa.

If I could make Gaugamela obey me like a cavalry, if the lines in the Twombly found all the verbs in Arrian, it would be a different kind of world. We could bandage our wounds with pages and talk to them like nervous horses into obedience. But nothing obeys me, and you have to pull out the barb of the sarissa stuck between your ribs or you'll die there, and Arrian or Xenophon or Cy Twombly aren't helping. You steal from them like a thief, like a lover who leaves in the morning they are not yours to keep.

There are no centaurs in Persia, and only men at Gaugamela. On the battlefield, it's all triage medicine.

4.

Here is the death of Hephaestion: it is a small thing close to the rightmost edge of the painting, a fainter grey than the battle because it almost flickers out. It looks like a candle with a hovering flame. There are either two or three things Alexander loved in all the world depending on your historical source: first his horse Bucephalus, gigantic and once afraid of his own shadow. Second, Hephaestion, with whom he lay wreaths on the tombs of Achilles and Patroclus at Troy, his other half. The third, if you take Plutarch's word and not Arrian's, if you maybe read the slightly purple gay novels of Mary Renault when you were fourteen, if you believe in the complexity of more or second love, and its chances— was a Persian eunuch named Bagoas. Actually, all that's in Plutarch is that he wins a dancing contest and the troops demand that Alexander kiss him.

I do not see Bagoas at all in *The Age Of Alexander*, but Twombly didn't see his future partner Nicola Del Roscio coming in 1959 either. He was happily married and expecting a son. His long affair with Rauschenberg was behind them. He had a beautiful apartment littered with antique busts in Rome; he even looks patrician and somehow still young in the 1960's photos. He was successful, to an extent. It is questionable whether history allows you to be both queer and successful, to unfurl your secret complexities and also live and be happy. That is too much to ask, apparently, for Alexander who is still unhappily conquering the world, and for Hephaestion, who dies after the troops make him march back from India, and a second time, into Babylon.

Alexander has made the army newly half Persian. Everybody takes a Persian bride. This is supposed to suture close Greece and Persians, the Lydians and the Athenians and the Medes, as if they could stop hating each other for being barbarians, as if conquest was a civilizing project, as if there even were sutures or the prospect of joining two wildly disparate and strange new things. Alexander learns Persian and the troops mutter. What happens when we become the thing we set out to conquer? If you try to make a Twombly your Twombly too much, it conquers you, and then you see it on your skin, on the body that you slip between two white sheets at night, in the absence of a human lover. It parasitizes you. You are an apple with a worm in it, digging into the core, dropping off a branch all Singer Sargent glowing in the autumn, but you know, you *know* you have been marked out somehow, tainted. Is it bad to be tainted?

When Hephaestion dies Alexander throws himself over

the body weeping and has to be pried off by force. *Do not talk to me about Achilles! Do not talk to me about Patroclus!* I say this but he says it too, in me, and in Arrian he is called disproportionate for cutting his hair like Achilles over the corpse. I cut my bangs in the sink, but I wanted to cut it all, to be disproportionate. He weeps for two days.

Arrian says the pyre on which he places the body to be burned has costly incense worth ten thousand talents. Diodorus describes the pyre too. A talent, which is a weight of coin measure totaling about 33 kg, is in today's money, worth about $1,400,000 USD. Ten talents are then 14 million US dollars. One of Twombly's chalkboard paintings sold at Christie's for about 69 million dollars, but the smaller paintings can sell for less. What is a life worth in talents? What is a Twombly worth?

I got a copy of the catalogue of *Fifty Days At Iliam* at the Gagosian Gallery in Grosvenor Square in London, when you could still go out to the Gagosian. I was wildly under-dressed and managed to get a damaged display copy for £50. You'd need 280,000 of them for a ten talent pyre. I still have the expensive black paper bag with the ribbon handles and the white sans-serif lettering with the gallery's name, on thick card stock nicer than my nicest stationery. Alexander also dies in Babylon not much later. Some say it was fever. Others, poisoning (*pharmakon*, maybe, too high a dose of Homeric Greek). I hold this paper bag, holding the sequence of the *Iliad* in fifty frames of paint and stare down at the glossy page with *The Age of Alexander* on it.

The flickering candle of Hephaestion's life is small against all the scribbled-out battles, the progress across the plain. But did it all matter after that?

I run in the park at midnight until dots appear in front of my eyes, until sine waves labeled 1-2-3-4 edge their way off the canvas. I vacuum the default-beige carpet of my flat until it is an unmarked picture plane. I cover it with an Afghan war carpet I found at a charity shop. It is rows and rows of grenades with the pins still in them, in a pattern that is traditionally a flower or a pomegranate. I scan the shelves that are a hanging garden, though I know I am not a bee that pollinates it but a mite eating at the root, or a grub, or a fly. I fall into it, stroking the spines like spears lined up, like the lip-edge of the above-world at the end of an anabasis. My legs don't know how to stop running back to the Aegean, how to stop climbing on up.

PART 5

"Who knows now what magic is:—the power to enchant /
That comes from disillusion. What books can teach one / Is
that most desires end up in stinking ponds..."

W. H. Auden, *The Sea And The Mirror:*
A Commentary on Shakespeare's Tempest,
from 'Prospero to Ariel'

1.

Before the re-exhibition of Cy Twombly's *Fifty Days At Iliam* at the Philadelphia Museum of Art in 2017, the Museum also received a related series of drawings called 'Shades of Night'. They were installed in a gallery near *Iliam*, five on one side, four on the other, with three Twombly sculptures in the middle. The sculptures consisted of one like the prow of an elongated Homeric black ship, as usual in monumental white paint, and two that seem like graves, one shaped like a traditional gravestone and the other a hoplite helmet. The 'Shades' are drawings all dual dated the same way on paper, visible above almost-floral blots of oil ranging from pure black to arterial red. The date is January 8, 1978 and August 1, 1978. This is far more than fifty days. The Shades themselves, those flower-blot-clouds, will crop up again in the war proper when important characters die, but here Twombly is studying grief as much as color.

What color is grief, then? I don't know; I did not last the fifty days of color study, much less the war. After only a lunar month the Girl Across the Sea and I spoke, gasping for each other's air. What we had learned in absence was that neither of us could bear it, that we would prefer to bear uncertainty, no oaths to be broken. Tissaphernes lives. Orpheus pauses and waits, reminding himself not to turn back. Two binary stars sink into each other's orbits and stay, even when one or the other goes supernova and collapses into a black hole, a blot cloud, a SHADE written with a capital Greek delta instead of an 'A.'

2.

If you had told me before that some affinities weren't elective, I would have laughed sadly. This was true in *literature. In art.* In the things I parasitized for certain. The wasp doesn't choose to need the fig, nor the tapeworm the gut. But Auden had prepared me for people, and Auden, well— do you remember the way nights of insult pass ("watched by every human love") in *Lullaby*, the way singular stars burn with an unreturnable passion ("If equal affection account be...") in *The More Loving One?* Auden had taught me that criticism is the only unconditional love, that you can love books and need books and art for certain, but people are fickle; they are not stars in any firmament. To love queerly, for Auden, was to prepare oneself to love painfully, evanescently, and perhaps not electively— but at least one could pretend the window dressing of need was a choice one could inoculate one-self against properly. His Prospero says it point blank:

"Who knows what magic is:— the power to enchant / That comes from disillusion. What books can teach one / Is that most desires end up in stinking ponds…"

The flooded Indus Valley with all Alexander's dying darlings was a stinking pond. Books taught me that. I made it an enchantment, I sung to my wounds. I prepared, having known them, to cast my books into the sea and learn to drink brack on an island of black-grey-red, shaped like a cloud, a flower, a last-hope raft, a Twombly Shade on the walls in Philadelphia.

3.

It turns out books are fickle too, that the insidious truth of art can also be a lie. I knew this, but evidently, I forgot or was rendered dumb in wanting. Reading back in order to read forward into the world is dangerous that way. The fish louse doesn't know any universe except the one inside the fish's mouth behind the teeth. Asking a fish louse to imagine a city or the Hubble Telescope would end badly. Asking the eye of the Hubble, trained on the birth nebulae of stars, to imagine the inside of a fish would end badly too. All eyes make false auguries sometimes, are conditioned to by their modes of being.

Ariel is not like Prospero. Ariel makes us rich and strange, and though pearls are not our eyes yet, the Girl Across the Sea and I coat the world in nacre for each other, re-enchant the disillusions and irritants into gems that spill out of our mouths onto paper and envelopes and correspondences. The Atlantic is not yet here the Aegean. Agamemnon doesn't drag his daughter to the altar in her saffron-yellow dress so the winds will fill his sails to Troy. Maybe someone eventually sends Nestor to a nursing home. He enjoys the craft hour, stringing together large plastic beads.

Even centaurs are, as even Auden is, wrong sometimes. We learn to drink the half-salt water and the swamp island is our own, and the sawgrass doesn't scrape when you run the right way with it against your legs, and we are crones waving our arms at the sky fitfully at lightning, during which we picnic, entirely and wildly unafraid.

4.

Eliot thinks the Sybil, in his Epigraph to *The Waste Land* from Petronius, wants to give up on living because schoolboys are throwing rocks at her:

> "Nam Sibyllam quidem Cumis ego ipse oculis meis vidi in ampulla pendere, et cum illi pueri dicerent: Σίβυλλα τι ἐλεις; respondebat illa: ἀπο θανείν θέλω."

> I saw with my own eyes the Sibyl at Cumae hanging in a cage, and when the boys said to her: "Sibyl, what do you want?" she answered: "I want to die."

The Sybil asked for eternal life but forgot to ask for eternal youth. She, herself, is ready to forget, has known enough and wants to cast her books into the sea, break her staff. She is an

Ariel worse than bound to a tree or a witch or a rightful Duke with too much free time. She sees the list Twombly has made in large graphite text of the Heroes of the Achaeans from *Fifty Days At Iliam*. She sees them every time she closes her eyes. MENELAUS. DIOMEDES. In red with capital deltas for 'As' again: ACHAENS ACHILLES. She knows the three shades on a white picture plane Achilles, Patroclus, Hector, blood-red, grey with a little ichor, graying white, all blooming sinister.

One night, with a gang of thieves, I sneak in and pick the lock on her cage with one of the sharp triangular points of the capital deltas. The door to the cage swings open, creaking. She smiles widely at the sea-change and bursts into a cloud of a thousand hundred *psenes*, little flies that will pester Centaurs until the heat death of the universe.

5.

I am listening to Telemann now, the harpsichord rings out into the night like bony, interlacing fingers. They are ivory, and so their dreams should be false. One of the things the Girl Across the Sea and I both love are the worlds painted on the inside of harpsichord lids. You could climb inside and live in them, the huge crags of rocks, the ruins, the blue of skies that is that particular Dutch early-modern blue, the color of an altarpiece afternoon with just a touch of green to it.

There is just the faintest echo of this blue in Twombly's *Shield of Achilles*, and more of it in the Thyrsis of Etna triptych. In the Shield it is mostly painted out, or around the edges of the scribbled whorl of oil crayon blue and black with a red paint core, writhing. Perhaps it has just come out of the furnace here, and only the thin edges have cooled. The shield is a whole world. Most of the eighteenth book of the *Iliad* is all a description of the shield, an ekphrasis, the first one that teaches us how ekphrasis should be for all of literature afterward. It is an act of critical appraisal wound inside the story itself, an egg waiting in the dark heart of the fig to become a brand new wasp. The *Iliad*'s disillusion with death and dying and endless war is still an enchantment, too.

Here, on the Shield, is the world Achilles will never live to go home to. Homer describes it like this: It has the moon and sun, the Pleiades and the Hyades glimmering in its sky. It has two cities; one teeming with people and quotidian acts of justice, purchase, wealth, crowds. The other city, like Troy, was under siege but proud, angered in bronze and gold. There is a fallow field in the moment of being ploughed in literal boustrophedon, and peasants sitting for a midday meal like Bruegel before the idea of Bruegel was ever born, and a sweet vineyard with young boys and girls, dancing. There is a herd of precious cattle, struggling to fend off a lion, and a shepherd's glade as peaceful as the cattle are harried. People dance and fall in joyous love. The river of the outer Ocean circles it all, a T-O map of everything that was and could be, and that Achilles, soon to die, would know now only in this image, only with his scanning eyes.

The Shield is a tender gift of mother to son, from Homer to reader or listener, whomever we imagine Homer to be. At the end of things, before you go out on the plain of Troy to throw yourself against the Scamander and the walls of Iliam, you can only listen, read, look, imagine for yourself what this means. In the second before he takes up his own flashing shield, before he strides to his death, Achilles too becomes, in a sense, a critic.

6.

One of the most moving paintings in the *Fifty Days At Iliam* series is "Achilles Mourning The Death Of Patroclus" which is just what Twombly writes on it and then crosses out, like x's for eyes, a transmogrified cartoon corpse on a bower. Achilles takes up his new shield only after Patroclus dies, wearing his armor, doing the favor to the Greeks he was too arrogant to do himself. Achilles hates himself for it.

Achilles says he loved Patroclus as he loved himself, his own soul. But who was the more loving one, the one left with Auden's unwavering, indifferent stars? It could go both ways, it cuts both ways, serrated and sharp.

This is φίλος—philos, a kind of love that doesn't exist in English truly, not for the quaverings of generations of phil-hellenic translations to make as plain as does the Greek, their Forsterian hesitations clumsy in the British Museum, hiding and revealing. It lives with *eros* but is not *eros* alone. Perhaps it is an *eros*, but only for clouds that are also souls.

In the painting, the Twombly of Achilles mourning Patroclus, two red scribbled clouds, joined by a single thin line of graphite pencil sit on that white, housepaint-ground of the mortal realm, on a canvas about my height, or that of a Bronze Age Greek warrior. Their helmets are so small in display cases and excavations, they could fit me instead, a little more than five feet tall. No wonder Ajax was a giant to them! In their world I fit.

One cloud, Achilles, is bright red, the kind of red that comes out when you slice near the aorta or pierce one of the big arteries connecting the legs with a mounted spear. The graphite scribble is under the oil, like a skeleton. The cloud that is Patroclus wanders up toward the right corner of the frame, connected only by the single fragile line. This wound-cloud is pinkish red, infiltrated by the white of winding cloths, already fading from the real. Another thin pencil line undercuts both clouds, as if to suggest they have already passed the gateway point for death, have begun katabasis, one following the other down. Once Patroclus dies, Achilles sees no reason to delay and live.

7.

In his description of the Shield, Auden blames Achilles. The last two lines of his poem on the subject are "Iron-hearted man-slaying Achilles / Who would not live long."

This is one of those rare moments when I rear up against Auden and disagree with him entirely. Would iron-hearted Achilles have wept and rent himself asunder, have bathed the corpse of Patroclus in honey and dressed its wounds? Would he have cut all his hair and thrown it into the pyre? An iron-hearted man wouldn't have cared, would have decided to live instead of die.

Twombly might blame Achilles too. Perhaps the most immediately striking painting in the *Iliam* series is titled "The Fire that Consumes All before it" and indeed, in a semi-currens scrawl, "like a fire that consumes all before it" is written on the canvas in red oil crayon. Most of the pictorial space is a central, red flame with a red heart where wick would be. This is the first word of the *Iliad*; "μῆνιν",the singular accusative of the word for rage—the rage of the son of Peleus, Achilles. And it does burn through the book like a fire, taking down bodies and hopes and reputations. Sometimes this is heartless.

Auden's Shield is more grisly than Homer's, more of a mirror than a map of possibility. In Auden's 'The Shield of Achilles,' Thetis expects to see what Homer describes, but the shield confounds her:

> She looked over his shoulder For
> vines and olive trees, Marble
> well-governed cities And ships
> upon untamed seas,
> But there on the shining metal His
> hands had put instead
> An artificial wilderness And
> a sky like lead.

The sky is lead, like I am white as lead, like I am dumb before need and beauty, but also cruelty. I'm a woman's lead, the lead that resists the myths of Updike's gods and whispers her secret own. Gods and men after all, are what we say are in contention here. Auden sees the armies for what they are, his witness of creeping fascism: "An unintelligible multitude / A million eyes, a million boots in line / Without expression, waiting for a sign." That was all Achilles needed to become a killing machine really, a sign, that's all Patroclus's death ultimately does in this bit of Auden. One cloud follows the other down because that's fate, not because that's love or *philos* or a tiny penciled line that is unbreakable even in dying, the orbits of perpetually twinned stars.

Auden also sees the Crucifixion prefigured on the shield. He sees a yammering crowd, a field ringed in barbed wire. Things as they truly are, stripped of oil, varnish, down to the white housepaint and graphite, a scene where:

> A ragged urchin, aimless and alone,
> Loitered about that vacancy; a bird
> Flew up to safety from his well-aimed
> stone: That girls are raped, that two boys
> knife a third, Were axioms to him, who'd
> never heard
> Of any world where promises were kept, Or
> one could weep because another wept.

I think this sometimes is our world, and the historical world of Homer too. It's the world where the tapeworm siphons off the nutrients from children in muddy hemispheric plots until they die of starvation. It's the malarial mosquito's world, the flies that swell the limbs with elephantiasis. It's a world that digs its *scolex* mouth into your flank until you scream in horror because you see it clearly.

But I weep still where another has wept, tears to salt a sea full of little stick-oar boats all sailing from Lepanto. If I collect my tears into a bowl, maybe my bones will change to coral.

8.

The thing is here — the thing that is the graphite line from that last section to this— is that Auden's wasps are not my wasps. His rage is not my rage. His shield is not my shield. I have climbed inside his voice like a well-worn blue cloak so many times now it is hard to say where he ends and I begin, but I can feel my human feet now where his hooves would be in this poem. I take his world but I take mine too, running in quantum parallel.

Yes, there is a rage that is the fire that consumes all that is before it. This is joy though too, the joy of seeing and reading and feeling things, of lover and beloved, that comes across the field of vision just as suddenly as that blot of red. Joy does this as much as rage, and sometimes with it in tow. Recall:

Loved him as he loved his own life.

Not for ten thousand talents.

"J'ai fait juste un bisou" !!!

"Who knows what magic is?" says Prospero to Ariel. But Ariel, who is pure magic, bound now only to air and sea—Ariel knows and works his changes, dipping in and out of a school of velveteen rays.

If Achilles is iron-hearted maybe I am too, swallowing it with my dinner. You must smelt iron to make bronze, after all. That too is axiomatic.

Rage can't obliterate memory, it just goes on over it, another coat of red until it becomes deeper to the eye. An egg is a memory of both the parasite that has already died to produce it, and the future of the host that will have it inside. Consider again the harpsichord keys of the tapeworm's proglottids, their potentiality in sequence for an exponential million times of fertile eggs. Consider the books on my living room shelves, each rectangular and next to the other; a key, a segment, a grin of teeth behind which the tongues of fishes and thieves lie in wait.

Consider a possible world where Achilles takes the other choice Thetis offers him in Book Nine; he runs away from being deployed to Troy and his mother does indeed hide him disguised as a dancing girl.

H. D.'s Helen stays in Egypt and launches a chain of successful wellness resorts for British expatriates. Her face stays beautiful for many years and lives to crinkle into lines when she smiles. The marbles of the Parthenon go back to Athens and the Athenians are still more Athenian than the rest of us about it, but all in good time.

Patroclus though, dies young of AIDS in 1986. Chiron could not cure him.

9.

This book is my Shield. You have seen it now; you are holding it by the leathern strap in the back as it faces out to meet its fate. I, too, will sneak away and become a dancing girl and live quietly and long. I will shout *tha-LASS-SA* at the sea, and *barbar* at visiting Greeks when they come. I will herd verses or sheep, and sit each night at the loom with the purple-red silk the Girl From Across the Sea ends me, just the color of murex and porphyry. I will dance to Telemann in a heatwave when I am taking out the trash. Point, Counterpoint: *loop loop loop*, the world turns on itself and I will dream it all in horn and will not be King of Macedon. My long disused-sarissa will prick the soil of the field where the oxen turn in ploughing. I will consume all that is before me, but I will burn instead of it, a Roman candle gone fire-Twombly-white. At night I will say the Eurydic rites before bed and scatter rose petals on the mosaic floor until their pattern appears in the tesserae. I will grow an extra set of legs, but stand in the back of the crowd and be amenable during the cocktail hour of Lapith weddings, even and especially to Updike.

I will unfurl my wet wings into the expectant space of the air, far from the nation of my birth, and fly, looking for the orchard and the fig trees, hung heavy with galls and with fruit.

A.V. Marraccini is a critic, essayist, and historian of art.

In addition to her scholarly work, she has written on both visual culture and literature for publications ranging from the *TLS* and the *LARB* to *BOMB* magazine and *Hyperallergic*. She is currently the critic in residence at the department of Interdisciplinary Media at NYU.

We The Parasites
By A. V. Marraccini

First published in this edition by Boiler House Press, 2023
Part of UEA Publishing Project
We The Parasites copyright © A. V. Marraccini

Editorial Coordination and Proofreading by James Hatton

Cover Design and Typesetting by Louise Aspinall
Typeset in Arnhem Pro & Garamond

ISBN: 978-1-915812-18-6